Endor

"Joan Masterson is appropriately living out her name. She is a masterful woman of God who is continually discovering new insights into Scripture, especially as it relates to the "One New Man" of Jew and Gentile united together as a divine proclamation of God's love story. I love the title of her book and its meaning for all of us - that Jesus' grandest joy is to dwell in the midst of a worldwide community of believers where His closest blood family the Jews, and the believers from the nations form one grand body of believers that draw others into the kingdom. Open your heart to Joan as she sits with you through the pages of her book, and receive the transforming insights that she brings. I wholeheartedly recommend this book to you."

— Don Finto
Caleb Global

"So honored to get a sneak peek into *Dwelling Place* by my friend, Joan Masterson. This has been a work in progress for some years, and I rejoice with her as it comes to fruition! Dwelling Place has been released in the fullness of time—as the Lord revealed revelation upon revelation to Joan's heart and now these revelations of "One New Man" have been transferred into print for us to explore. As you read through its pages, you will actually find yourself in the midst of a conversation with Joan— a gifted storyteller, who tells The Greatest Story ever told. She shares her own personal journey, as a friend would share over coffee, combined with sharing Biblical truths as a gifted teacher of the Word of God. Thank you for staying the course, Daughter of Zion, and for sharing your revelation, gift of storytelling, and most of all, your love of Yeshua/Jesus, with all of us!"

— Christine Vales
Teacher and Author of *His Appointed Times:*
Uncovering the Lord's Prophetic Calendar in Real-Time
www.christinevales.com

"I feel like the biblical teachings are clear, thorough and revelatory."

— Robyn Vincent
Glory of Zion International

Dwelling Place is a must read for anyone who is trying to figure out where they fit in God's big plan. He longs for sons and daughters to come home to sit as His table and learn of His ways.

Written from the heart of a Jewish believer who has lived through her identity crisis, this book makes incredible sense as it delivers a very real picture of Ephesian's "One New Man" the dwelling place of God in the Spirit among His Jewish and Gentile Children."

— Juliann Gregory
Aligned with Heaven Inc

Dwelling Place is a wonderful book that ministers to both serious students of the Bible as well as new believers. Joan has a compelling writing style … her "heart" shines through on every page. In our day of rising anti-Semitism, this book is an important addition, reminding us of the One New Man that Messiah Jesus has purchased by His shed blood on the cross."

— Barbi and Terry Franklin, Nashville TN
www.WorshipCity.com

"I'm honored to call Joan Masterson my friend. This book allows you to access her amazing ability to see truth through her love of God's heart. The phrase "God's heart" recurs throughout, because that Heart is the motivation of her life. You will be shocked at the truths she presents about the foundations of "Fulfillment Theology." She stringently but kindly smacks those who err on this subject, but not only that—she calls those of us "enlightened" ones to be careful lest we also fall! Prepare to face your own heart in her writing. I highly recommend it!"

— Rev. Carolyn Parr
Sing Your Song Ministries
www.carolynparr.com

Dwelling Place

Dwelling Place

GOD'S ENDTIME STRATEGY
A DWELLING PLACE FOR HIMSELF
IN THE HEARTS
OF HIS SONS AND DAUGHTERS

Joan Masterson

TIKVAH PUBLISHING

Joan Masterson/Tikvah Publishing Company™
Post Office Box 143
Thompsons Station, Tennessee 37179
www.tikvahpublishing.com

Unless otherwise indicated, all Scripture quotations are taken from the (NASB®) New American Standard Bible®, Copyright © 1960, 1971, 1977, 1995, 2020 by The Lockman Foundation. Used by permission. All rights reserved. www.Lockman.org.

Scripture quotations marked AMP taken from the Amplied® Bible, Copyright © 2015 by the Lockman Foundation. Used by Permission. www.lockman.org

Scripture quotations marked AMPC taken from the Amplied® Bible, Copyright © 1954, 1958, 1962, 1964, 1965, 1987 by The Lockman Foundation. Used by permission. www.lockman.org

Scripture quotations marked NLT are from the Holy Bible, New Living Translation, copyright © 1996, 2004, 2007, 2013, 2015 by Tyndale House Foundation. Used by permission of Tyndale House Publishers, Inc., Carol Stream, Illinois 60188. All rights reserved.

Scripture quotations marked KJV are taken from the King James Version of the Bible. Public domain.

Scripture quotations marked NKJV are from the New King James Version.® Copyright ©1982 by Thomas Nelson, Inc. Used by permission. All rights reserved.

Scripture quotations marked MSG are from THE MESSAGE, copyright © 1993, 2002, 2018 by Eugene Peterson. Used by permission by NavPress, represented by Tyndale House Publishers. All rights reserved.

Scripture quotations marked PNT are taken from The Power New Testament, copyright © 2003 William J. Morford. Used by permission of True Potential Publishing, Inc.

Scripture quotations marked CJB are taken from the Complete Jewish Bible by David H. Stern. Copyright ©1998. All rights reserved. Used by permission of Messianic Jewish Publishers. www.messianicjewish.net

Dwelling Place / Joan Masterson —1st ed.
ISBN 978-0-9906213-7-9

Edited by Ann Severance - Annwsev@att.net
Edited by Linda Hogan - 365wordsmiths@gmail.com
Book Cover and Interior Layout Design by: Melissa Staff - redtulipcreative.com

Table of Contents

For God so loved the world, that He gave His only begotten Son, that whoever believes in Him shall not perish, but have eternal life. ~ John 3:16

How did this Jewish author meet her Jewish Messiah?
Answers the age-old question: Why the Jewish people anyway?

I do not ask on behalf of these alone, but for those also who believe in Me through their word; that they may all be one; even as You, Father, are in Me and I in You, that they also may be in Us, so that the world may believe that You sent Me. ~ John 17:20-21

Study of Ephesians 2: Biblical explanation of the One New Man and God's dwelling place.
Father God created through the work of the cross One New Man – to satisfy the prayer of Yeshua/Jesus (John 17).

Therefore remember that formerly you, the Gentiles in the flesh, were at that time separate from Christ, excluded from the commonwealth of Israel, and strangers to the covenants of promise, having no hope and without God in the world. ~ Ephesians 2:11a-12

The restoration of what was lost in the Garden; a dwelling place where God can have fellowship with man.

CHAPTER EIGHT

The Great Deception

We are destroying arguments and all arrogance raised against the knowledge of God, and we are taking every thought captive to the obedience of Christ.~ 2 Corinthians 11:25

Teachings on "Replacement Theology".

CHAPTER NINE

The Evidence

If someone says, "I love God," and yet he hates his brother or sister, he is a liar; for the one who does not love his brother and sister whom he has seen, cannot love God, whom he has not seen. ~ 1 John 4:20

History of the evidence of replacement theory and the roots of anti-Semitism is very painful. Even greater is the pain that today the evidence continues in our current society globally.

Acknowledgements

Without a doubt, the Holy Spirit wrote this book. I am just a scribe.

For me to thank all the people by name who prayed for me through these last three years to finish this book, would take up an entire chapter. So many have encouraged me and believed in this project from the very start. It is with my heartfelt gratitude that I express my love for all they contributed.

All production aspects of this book have been brought forth with excellence by my dear friend and sister in the Lord, Melissa Staff. She not only readied the manuscript for print and created the cover. She has taken on every aspect of marketing and I would not know what to do with out her expertise.

A special thanks goes to Linda Hogan who came in as we got ready to cross the finish line as my second editor.

But one person stands out in particular. The truth is without the love and confidence building that she offered me, along with her excellence as an editor, you would not be holding this book in your hands right now. I am thankful that God gave me the privilege of knowing and working with Anne Severance. My beloved, Ann, is not only an extraordinary editor, I'm honored to call her a dear friend and sister in the Lord. Just at the right time, God sent me this heavenly gift.

Sometimes she served as my mentor, other times as my coach, and on any given day, as a cheerleader, keeping me going through the production of this book. Ann truly embodies the essence of this verse: "Friends come and friends go, but a true friend sticks by you like family." Proverbs 18:24 *(MSG)*

Foreword

When Janet and I first met Joan Masterson, she presented herself in an introductory email as "Grandma Joan," who God had told to organize a Jewish roots conference and asked me to be the main speaker. She told me she knew nothing about doing this but was willing to "step out of her boat and walk on water." I loved that!!

I immediately recognized in Joanie the heart of an authentic disciple of the Kingdom and this drew me to her. Over the ensuing years, as I have walked with her as a friend and mentor, I have had the pleasure of watching her go from "Grandma Joan" to a minister, teacher, and leader in the Body of Christ. I have watched her take on assignments that made her follow in the steps of the "faith of Abraham" (Romans 4:12). No matter what obstacles she faced, she did not back down but overcame. She will receive the reward of an overcomer!

Out of this heart to listen and obey, Joanie took on the assignment to author this book. Discovering the ability to write, she has given a gift to the Church and the Jewish people. In these pages, you will find many Biblical truths to not only learn but be challenged to ask yourself about your place in God's ultimate plan of redemption. What will you do with what you learn?

My prayer is that the Lord will use this book to stimulate study and discussion into the important issues Joanie has raised. You may not agree with all you read, but I hope it will spur you to ask yourself, what do you really believe, and again, what are you doing about it?

May we all be maturing fruitful disciples of the Kingdom of God!

Dr. Howard Morgan
Kingdom Ministries Inc.
www.kingmin.org

Introduction

My journey to understanding the "One New Man" as a Jewish believer began over twenty years ago. It has indeed been a walk of revelation upon revelation, and one significant revelation led to the title of this book, *Dwelling Place*.

No doubt you thought *Dwelling Place* is a strange title for a book about the One New Man. Me, too! Not until you can understand that the One New Man is God's eternal end game plan can you grasp the full scope of the heart of God. It was in the final verses of Ephesians 2 that God revealed the depth of His heart to me. In this chapter you find the only place in our Bible that uses the words *one new man*. Here He showed me that the desire of His heart is to have a Dwelling Place in the Spirit for Himself on earth.

That Dwelling Place was to be built upon the foundation of the Prophets and the Apostles, with Jesus the Cornerstone. That Dwelling Place in the Spirit is the Commonwealth of Israel. The Commonwealth of Israel is comprised of Jews and Gentiles functioning in the Spirit through Yeshua Jesus as the One New Man.

In light of that, through the pages of this book, I have attempted to present God's eternal plan for mankind—from Genesis to Revelation, The Great Deceptions that Satan has used from the Garden until now, and a biblical picture of what I have learned about the One New Man and your role in it.

As you join me on my journey of discovery, my sincere hope is that you won't acquire *information* but *impartation*, from the heart of the Father through the Holy Spirit. Just as the earth is groaning for the manifestation of the sons of God, so is the Father. The

One New Man is just that—the manifestation of the sons—and daughters—of God.

The pages of this book hold a great deal more than just that understanding for in the process of God fulling our destiny He has laid out a blue print for the building of the Kingdom of God and my journey has highlighted many aspect of that on my road to discovery.

The importance of the role of the Prophets and the Apostles is finally coming to light in the Body of Christ. On the Hebrew calendar, 5780 that began on; our Gregorian Calendar on September 30 ,2019, it is considered "The Year of the Mouth". Thus the year of the mouth is the year of declaration in the Hebrew culture. On January 1, 2020, we began a new era, with an emphasis for the *Ekklesia* to step up through agreement and declaration of God's Word to establish His will on earth as it is in heaven.

In the New Testament, the word church comes originally from the word *Ekklesia* which, by definition, means the called-out ones and a legislative body with Yeshua Jesus as the Head.

> *For a child will be born to us, a son will be given to us; And then government will rest on His shoulders; And His name will be called Wonderful Counselor, Mighty God, Eternal Father, Prince of Peace.*
>
> ~ Isaiah 9:6

Permit me to share part of an encounter I had with the Lord as He called me to intercede for our nation in 2016. Immediately, my eyes were drawn upward to a very large book, open in heaven. Bound in brown leather, the book was old, but not ancient. I knew by the Spirit that its pages contained God's will for America.

I cried out, "Abba, how do we get Your will in heaven established on the earth?"

This was His reply: *I will send My will through My messenger angels to the prophetic platform speakers and the prophetic intercessors and, as the Ekklesia comes into agreement with and declares My will as one voice, it will be established on earth as it is in heaven.*

As biblical confirmation of my encounter in the year 2020, the Lord then pointed out to me the following Scripture, which bears the numbers 2020.

> *Jehoshaphat stood and said, "Listen to me, O Judah and inhabitants of Jerusalem, put your trust in the LORD your God and you will be established. Put your trust in His prophets and succeed."*
>
> ~ 2 Chronicles 20:20

As I hear frequently these days: *"You can't make this stuff up!"*

In this present day—the beginning of a new decade—we need a clear understanding of the voice of God through His chosen vessels and the will of God given us from His Word. Dear reader, if we do *not* have a clear understanding of where Israel and the Jewish people fit into this end-time scenario, we will fall prey to deception, which we have been warned about by Jesus Himself.

So I pray as you follow me through these pages, He will enlarge your boundaries in pleasant places and you will see how exciting it is to be born for such a time as this.

Dear Reader,

Thank you for choosing to read my book. My desire was to write this book as though you and I are sitting in my living room face to face, sharing our hearts and exploring our questions together. From the endorsements I have received, God has faithfully helped me fulfill that desire. I have taught classes via conference calls for over 20 years with that same format in mind. Students throughout the nation call in weekly for interactive learning.

Throughout these pages, you will see that I have quoted friends and ministry leaders that I have the privilege to know. None of us have all the answers. That is why we are called the Body of Christ. We need to work together with the giftings and understanding God has entrusted to each of us. Together, with His Word and His Spirit, we have a broader scope of the counsel of God.

As you read this book, I encourage you to email me if you have questions. If I don't have an answer, I will point you in the direction of someone I think may be able to help.

Thanks again for joining me on the journey,

Joanie

Joanie@JoanMasterson.com

For God so loved the world, that
He gave His only begotten Son, that
whoever believes in Him shall not
perish, but have eternal life.

~John 3:16

1

THE BIG PICTURE

IN THE LEARNING PROCESS of what it meant to be a believing Jew in the Body of Christ, I heard consistently that no one really knows what the One New Man looks like. Seasoned forerunners of this message presented it as a mystery yet to be unfolded.

From the beginning, however, each teacher made it clear that the One New Man is a union of Jewish and Gentile believers. These individuals, either Jew or Gentile, believed that Yeshua (Jesus' Hebrew name) was sent by God to redeem mankind. For the sake of clarity, we need to understand that the word *Gentile* encompasses all other nations and nationalities.

Now, twenty years later, I believe that I can scripturally draw you a picture of the process and the plan that God has laid out in His Word. He graciously placed passages throughout the entire Bible that substantiate His ultimate plan of love. That plan is stated in the most well-known passage of Scripture:

For God so loved the world, that He gave His only begotten Son, that whoever believes in him shall not perish, but have eternal life.

~ John 3:16, KJV

What does "eternal life" mean to you? To God, it means He wants to spend forever and always with you. That was the original plan when He created Adam and Eve. God gave the first couple the ability to birth eternal beings to enjoy fellowship with God and with each other. In the Garden when Satan deceived Adam and Eve, they lost that privilege. (see Genesis 3) His plan was to destroy that fellowship and position them in eternal separation from God.

Growing Up Jewish in a Gentile Neighborhood

My family—Mom, Dad, and me, their infant daughter—resided in a garden apartment home in a small town in New Jersey, where we were the only Jewish residents. It was a typical suburban community with tree-lined streets and houses, each with a distinct style of construction.

Homeowners were very invested in their homes and their well-manicured lawns, which helped my parents' business, a hardware store catering to home maintenance, decorating, and lawn care. In the early years, Dad was a Merchant Marine and would take trips to bring in extra money needed to support the store until the business was built up. As time went on, the business did very well. With its potbelly stove, captain's chairs, and checkerboard table, providing a place for the men of the community to share tips about their lawn upkeep and housing projects. The store became a memorable part of the community. So, as not to leave out the women, my mom opened an area for crafters and gift items.

For a few years, Mom and Dad had a huge Christmas assortment of trains and other toys for purchase, which were displayed in the store adjacent to ours until a children's clothing store took over that space. My fondest memory was the music that played from a loudspeaker above the front door, ringing out Christmas songs for the shoppers. As I look back, I think how strange that the only Jewish family in town was making a point to celebrate the season with their Gentile friends. Perhaps it was my parents' way of fitting in.

Sadly, my mom became a widow when cancer took the life of my father. I was seven. After that, we bought a home on one of those quiet streets near the hardware store; my mom continued to be the sole proprietor.

A neighbor on my street had a beautiful collie. Our family pet was a dog of variety. She and I began to walk our dogs together daily. On those walks, she shared Bible stories with me. One summer when I was eleven, she asked my mom if she could treat me to a week at camp.

That camp was Jack Wyrtzen's Word of Life Baptist Camp. It was there I had a life-changing encounter with God and gave my heart to Jesus. Even at age eleven, I knew I wanted to spend forever with the One who had created me. I met Him first as my Savior.

I always wondered if Mom was ever told or if she even asked what kind of camp it was. I do know when I returned home and told her I would pray for her, it was the only time in my life she ever hit me. She broke two blood vessels in my leg. However, the God encounter was real, and nothing changed my confidence in my commitment. In the closing chapter of my mother's life, she came to know the Lord, too. It is a beautiful story for another time or perhaps another book.

A few weeks after camp, I found myself accompanying my dog-walking friend to her church, where I was baptized. Looking back, I realize it was a Pentecostal church. As I was in the water, I remember a little elderly man in the congregation standing up and saying,

"Daughter of Zion, someday you will lead many of your people to the Lord."

How odd, I thought. *Did someone tell him I was Jewish? They certainly tell me I don't look Jewish.* I do remember at the sound of his voice, the water seemed to begin to wave unusually. I can still see his face—a sweet, gray-haired grandfatherly type.

This was the beginning of my calling—a calling I did not acknowledge, one that did not take shape until my adult life. Immediately, though, I began to love the Word. I slept with my Bible under my pillow each night and read it constantly. One day shortly after my baptism, I asked the Lord what He wanted me to do with my life. Opening my Bible at the end of my prayer, my eyes fell on the following Scripture, which I then underlined in red and dated. Somehow, I knew this was another encounter with the Lord.

> *I solemnly charge you in the presence of God and of Christ Jesus, who is to judge the living and the dead, and by His appearing and His kingdom: preach the word; be ready in season and out of season; reprove, rebuke, exhort, with great patience and instruction. For the time will come when they will not endure sound doctrine; but wanting to have their ears tickled, they will accumulate for themselves teachers in accordance to their own desires, and will turn away their ears from the truth and will turn aside to myths. But you, be sober in all things, endure hardship, do the work of an evangelist, fulfill your ministry.*
>
> ~ 2 Timothy 4:1-5

Interesting to note that forty-nine years later at age 60, when I was ordained, by Dr. Howard Morgan, an internationally known Messianic Jewish leader, he read that very scripture. Dr. Morgan had no knowledge that what he read was what the Lord had spoken to His eleven-year-old daughter as she lay across her bed that day.

Although my walk with the Lord began at age eleven, it was not until I was in my fifties that I understood that Jesus was my Jewish Messiah. At that time God provided me with the following encounter with Jesus.

In an open vision, Jesus, dancing in a tallit[1], appeared to me. He reached out to me and addressed me as "Esther." Jesus knew my name was "Joan," yet that day He was identifying my calling, and confirming my bloodline, and ultimately my part in the Body of Messiah. I looked into His loving eyes, which seemed to sparkle, and I found myself exclaiming, "Oh, you really *are* Jewish!" His smile was endearing. That moment began a journey that has enabled me to write the pages of this book.

Many in the Church today have yet to experience the fullness of that revelation. I get it; for most of my time in the Church, the importance of the Jewishness of Jesus was simply not mentioned if it were grasped at all. I knew that when Jesus was here on Earth, He was Jewish, but when He ascended to Heaven as the risen Lord, I never again thought of Him as Jewish. Nor did I consider that He would be coming back as a Jew to rule as King of kings from Jerusalem.

So ... Why the Jew Anyway?

Why are the Jews, as a people group, separated out from all other nations? Why, if you are a non-Jewish believer, should you care about the Jewish people? Why did God go to such extremes to point out His covenantal ways through these particular people? Why did He choose to bring His Son into this world as a Jew and later to return as a Jew?

1 Tallit is a prayer shawl with fringed corners worn over the head or shoulders by Jewish men especially during morning prayers. Merriam-Webster.com Dictionary, s.v. "tallit," accessed February 17, 2021, https://www.merriam-webster.com/dictionary/tallit.

A condensed answer to those questions is: Through one man–Abraham, God created a people group from the existing humanity on planet Earth to reveal His heart, His ways, and His Son. That was how God would relay His plan of redemption to the world He loved.

That people group we now call the Jewish people is His very costly gift to the nations and hold a special place in His heart because of the purpose for which He created them. He expects us to care for that gift correctly.

> *He says, "It is too small a thing that You should be My Servant To raise up the tribes of Jacob and to restore the preserved ones of Israel; I will also make You a light of the nations So that My salvation may reach to the end of the earth."*
>
> ~ Isaiah 49:6

The following Scripture is a beautiful picture of God's love and loyalty to His Word and YOU. He points out to the Jewish people that He chose them not because of their great size or ability, but simply because of His love and faithfulness to those who chose to love Him and keep covenant with Him.

> *For you are a holy people to the LORD your God; the LORD your God has chosen you to be a people for His own possession out of all the peoples who are on the face of the earth.*
>
> *The LORD did not set His love on you nor choose you because you were more in number than any of the peoples, for you were the fewest of all peoples, but because the LORD loved you and kept the oath which He swore to your forefathers, the LORD brought you out by a mighty hand and redeemed you from the house of slavery, from the hand of Pharaoh king of Egypt.*

Know therefore that the LORD your God, He is God, the faithful God, who keeps His covenant and His lovingkindness to a thousandth generation with those who love Him and keep His commandments.

~ Deuteronomy 7:6-11

Initially, the people group that God chose was called the Hebrews, which means "the ones who crossed over." The Hebrews were later called Israelites and, eventually, the Jewish people. Throughout the generations, they have maintained the record of their relationship with God and the history of their land—Israel—on which God put His name.

Through this inspired record in what most call the Old Testament of the Bible, written by men under the anointing of the Holy Spirit, God teaches us how to relate to Him and each other. Additionally, this record gives us instructions concerning the blessings of obedience and the consequences of disobedience. Most importantly, we learn His plan of salvation in the coming of Messiah, first as Servant and then as King.

I have come to call the Old Testament the "Foundational Testament." Some consider, when thinking of these writings as "old," that they are obsolete and that the new writings replace the old. The truth is the New Testament writings are solely based on the Old Testament. Jesus and the apostles quoted exclusively from them in all their teachings. The New Testament teachings are actually like a commentary on what God had given as a foundation of His ways.

As we study together, keep in mind these concepts: sonship, adoption, and dwelling place for God. If you truly want to understand God's end-time plan, then grasping the fullness of Ephesians 2 and Romans 11 is a key to His heart. He longs for sons and daughters to sit at His table and learn of His ways, thus restoring the fellowship He enjoyed with His created beings in the Garden before the Fall.

The Picture Book

The statement "a picture is worth a thousand words" is quite true. Through the story of the Jewish people, God has given us a "picture book" so we might more fully comprehend His plan of salvation. As we ponder that reality, we can understand why God's enemy, Satan, has worked so hard to destroy and devalue them as a people. His ultimate goal is to keep the clarity of God's plan hidden.

If, in fact, the Jewish people are a picture book to reveal God's plan to us, the introduction to their book is recorded in Genesis 3. Here we learn the story of the Fall of man and God's plan of redemption. God tells Satan that the seed of the woman will crush Satan's head.

Yet, although the introduction prepares us for a story to unfold, God does not initially tip us off to His strategy. Remember, Eve was not a Hebrew or an Israelite or even what we now call Jewish. It was not until later when God calls Abram out of his pagan culture and gives him some phenomenal promises, that His strategy begins to unfold.

First, He calls Abram to be the father of a nation not yet established:

> *Now the LORD said to Abram, "Go forth from your country, and from your relatives, and from your father's house, to the land which I will show you; and I will make you a great nation, and I will bless you, and make your name great; and so you shall be a blessing; and I will bless those who bless you, and the one who curses you I will curse. And in you all the families of the earth will be blessed."*
>
> ~ Genesis 12:1-3

Here in bold type, God is declaring His plan for the salvation of the world. "For God so LOVED *the world*" (John 3:16).

May I point out here the importance of studying the Word in the language in which it was originally written? When we examine the meanings of the words in Hebrew, we come away with a fuller understanding of what God was presenting to Abram.

In the Genesis passage, the word *bless* means far more than just "to do good." It means "to honor, to bow low." Also, in that Scripture, the first Hebrew word for *curse* means "to take for granted" as well as to "treat lightly or without honor." However, the second word for *curse* is "to do harm; to literally bring a curse upon them." God was warning us not to take for granted those who would come from the promised sons of Abraham.

Ah ... and now we see, too, that Satan took God at His word and hatched his own plan to stir up hatred against the Jewish people—a hatred that would last for millennia. A hatred that would cause a curse on many nations.

In the Genesis 12 passage, God shows us the role of the Jewish people—to be a blessing to the world; the role of the Gentiles—to honor that blessing. The blessing that would come through Abram would be a race of people that continued through Isaac, the promised son, and then through Jacob. (Notice in the following passage that God has changed Abram's name to Abraham to reflect his ultimate calling. Abram, in Hebrew, means "exalted father"; Abraham means "father of a multitude.")

> *Then God said to Abraham, "As for Sarai your wife, you shall not call her name Sarai, but Sarah shall be her name. I will bless her, and indeed I will give you a son by her. Then I will bless her, and she shall be a mother of nations; kings of peoples will come from her."*
>
> *Then Abraham fell on his face and laughed, and said in his heart, "Will a child be born to a man one hundred years old? And will Sarah, who is ninety years old, bear a child?*

And Abraham said to God, "Oh that Ishmael might live before You!" But God said, "No, but Sarah your wife will bear you a son, and you shall call his name Isaac; and I will establish My covenant with him for an everlasting covenant for his descendants after him.

"As for Ishmael, I have heard you; behold, I will bless him, and will make him fruitful and will multiply him exceedingly. He shall become the father of twelve princes, and I will make him a great nation. But My covenant I will establish with Isaac, whom Sarah will bear to you at this season next year."

~ Genesis 17:15-22

God heard the request of Abraham and agreed to bless Ishmael. Faithful to His Word, God blessed the descendants of Ishmael in number and wealth. Please keep in mind that they are the Arabic peoples, not necessarily Muslim. Some have become Christians, and today there is a mighty awakening in the Middle East as thousands are coming to the Lord. God loves the descendants of Ishmael; however, He chose to make His covenant with Isaac.

That fact is one we may not fully understand. However, as God reminded Job, we are limited in understanding His ways:

"Where were you when I laid the foundation of the earth? Tell Me, if you have understanding."

~ Job 38:4

Again, in the book of Isaiah, He explains:

"For My thoughts are not your thoughts, nor are your ways My ways," declares the LORD. "For as the heavens are higher than the earth, so are My ways higher than your ways and My thoughts than your thoughts."

~ Isaiah 55:8-9

The people group from Isaac and eventually his son, Jacob—God changed his name to Israel—would be a light to the nations to reveal God's eternal plan.

But thou, Israel, art my servant, Jacob whom I have chosen, the seed of Abraham my friend.

~ Isaiah 41:8

The Apple of His Eye

Through the years, those with a heart for Israel and the Jewish people have emphasized that God's people are the "apple of His eye":

For thus says the LORD of hosts, "After glory He has sent me against the nations which plunder you [Israel], for he who touches you, touches the apple of His eye."

Zechariah 2:8

The "apple" is pictured as the pupil or lens from which one sees clearly. God is warning: "Don't touch the lens!" When we look through His lens, the picture book of Israel, it is only then that we can clearly distinguish the revelations of His heart.

When you begin to understand things from a Hebraic perspective, it is not wise to add that understanding to what you know, but rather to use your new understanding as the lens or filter to see if what you know is what God *intended*. Never forget that all of this is to reveal God's love for you and that He chose the Jewish people to show you the extent of that love, even to giving up His Son on the cross for your sin.

The people coming from Abraham's line were not without responsibility. They were chosen for a purpose, one of which was to keep careful records of God's instructions and their relationship with

God and with each other. Their records found in the Torah[2] given to Moses contain the Ten Commandments and other instructions for living, the covenants, and the temple sacrifices. These were instructions for drawing near to God and ultimately revealing the work of the cross. Contained within those writings is the calendar of God explaining the *Moedim*[3] or "Feasts of the Lord," further translated as "the appointed times of the Lord." Let us be clear: these are not times of the Jewish people. God chose the Jewish people to show us how God would have us celebrate His goodness: however, these are times of historic remembrance, times of present fellowship with the Father, and rehearsals of a time yet to come.

Within the first five books of the Bible (referred to today as the Pentateuch), as well as the Prophets and Poetry books of the Old Testament, is contained the history of the Jewish people. These reveal more about covenantal relationships, the prophetic destiny of all nations, and the ongoing revelation of the coming Messiah.

These books also give an accurate account of the Jewish people's shortcomings as well as their obedience, describing the consequences or rewards of each behavior. Throughout, God expresses His heart of love, His eternal faithfulness, and all His ways through the means of instruction.

Later, in the New Testament, Yeshua stated that He had only come to the lost sheep of the House of Israel (see Matthew 15:24). He had also sent the original twelve followers only to the House of Israel (see Matthew 10:6). Why? Because they were to be the carriers of His Word to the rest of the world—a "light to the Nations."

God's plan was *always* for the whole world to be redeemed, and He chose the Hebrews through whom to accomplish His purpose.

---

[2] Torah in Hebrew means teaching or instruction, not law. It is most often considered as the first five books in the Jewish Bible.

[3] In Hebrew, Moedim means "Feasts of the Lord" or God's "appointed times" (Leviticus 23).

After these things I looked, and behold, a great multitude which no one could count, from every nation and all tribes and peoples and tongues, standing before the throne and before the Lamb, clothed in white robes, and palm branches were in their hands; and they cry out with a loud voice, saying, "Salvation to our God who sits on the throne, and to the Lamb."

And all the angels were standing around the throne and around the elders and the four living creatures; and they fell on their faces before the throne and worshiped God, saying, "Amen, blessing and glory and wisdom and thanksgiving and honor and power and might, be to our God forever and ever. Amen."

~ Revelation 7: 9-12

In all this, it was revealed that every nation and every tribe will honor the God of Israel. God of whom? God of Israel. Why? Because Israel is where His throne will be. Why did Yeshua's/Jesus' death and resurrection take place in Israel? It is the land where God has placed His name.

"But to his son I will give one tribe, that My servant David may have a lamp always before Me in Jerusalem, the city where I have chosen for Myself to put My name."

~ 1 Kings 11:36

* * *

Israel is the land of God's picture book. Even today, it is the picture of what the hearts of mankind reveal. God also uses Israel and the Jewish people to reveal *your* heart. Do *you* love what God loves? *Selah.*

Why, in God's Word, does He say He is calling the Jewish people home to Israel? Because God started the story there and He will finish the story there. It was Jesus Himself who said:

"Jerusalem, Jerusalem, who kills the prophets and stones those who are sent to her! How often I wanted to gather your children together, the way a hen gathers her chicks under her wings, and you were unwilling. Behold, your house is being left to you desolate! For I say to you, from now on you will not see Me until you say, 'BLESSED IS HE WHO COMES IN THE NAME OF THE LORD!'"

~ Matthew 23:37-39

The final chapter of planet Earth will not be played out until the Jewish firstborn of Israel says, "Blessed is He who comes in the Name of the Lord."

Dear Reader, the Gentiles have a huge part to play in this. Just as a Gentile had a huge part to play in my life by sharing the Gospel with me and being part of what my friend, Tod McDowell[4] calls "the cycle of revival" and I call "the level playing field." You will learn more about this when we study Romans 11 (see Chapter 7). Stay tuned.

---

[4] Tod McDowell is executive director of Caleb Global, a missional Jesus-centered ministry. Its mission is to ignite revival in Israel, the Middle East, and the nations. For more information, visit: https://caleb.global.

For through Him we both
[Jew and Gentile] have our access in one
Spirit to the Father. So then you are no
longer strangers and aliens, but you are
fellow citizens with the saints and are of
God's household.

~ Ephesians 2:18-19 [author insertion]

2

THE PLAN

One New Man Equals One New Humanity

WHEN GOD, THROUGH ABRAHAM, first created a people group, He gave to the world the Jewish people to reveal the coming of Yeshua/Messiah. Centuries later, through Yeshua's/Jesus' sacrificial work on the cross, Father God created another new humanity, or One New Man—this time to satisfy the prayer of Yeshua/Jesus in John 17:

"I do not ask on behalf of these alone, but for those also who believe in Me through their word; that they may all be one; even as You, Father, are in Me and I in You, that they also may be in Us, so that the world may believe that You sent Me."

~ John 17:20-21

All of mankind was to be invited into the Father's household. No one was to be left out—unless they chose to be! And there was—and still is—that choice. Still, God's Plan was all-inclusive. Always has been. Always will be.

In my desire to share the full Word of God with you, I have put together the passages that express His heart on this important subject. Therefore, here is The Plan in its entirety from God's own inspired words through Paul:

> *And He came and preached peace to you who were far away, and peace to those who were near; for through Him we both [Jew and Gentile] have our access in one Spirit to the Father. So then you are no longer strangers and aliens, but you are fellow citizens with the saints [Jews], and are of God's household, having been built on the foundation of the apostles and prophets, Christ Jesus Himself being the cornerstone, in whom the whole building, being fitted together, is growing into a holy temple in the Lord, in whom you also are being built together into a dwelling of God in the Spirit.*

> ~ Ephesians 2:17-22 [author insertion]

Origin of The Plan

In the Garden of Eden, when Satan deceived Adam and Eve, they lost the privilege of eternal fellowship with God. However, God's Plan from the very beginning was to redeem mankind from that fatal sin. That is why the Bible tells us that Jesus was crucified "before the foundation of the world."

In 1 Peter, we find a verse that reinforces the truth of the origin of God's Plan:

> *If you address as Father the One who impartially judges according to each one's work, conduct yourselves in fear during the time of*

your stay on earth; knowing that you were not redeemed with perishable things like silver or gold from your futile way of life inherited from your forefathers, but with precious blood, as of a lamb unblemished and spotless, the blood of Christ.

For He was foreknown before the foundation of the world, but has appeared in these last times for the sake of you who through Him are believers in God, who raised Him from the dead and gave Him glory, so that your faith and hope are in God.

~ 1 Peter 1: 17-21

And, again, in Revelation, we read:

All who dwell on the earth will worship him, everyone whose name has not been written from the foundation of the world in the book of life of the Lamb who has been slain.

~ Revelation 13:8

The book of Matthew gives us a glimpse of the truth that, beyond salvation, God's heart was to build His Kingdom:

Then the King will say to those on His right, "Come, you who are blessed of My Father, inherit the kingdom prepared for you from the foundation of the world."

~ Matthew 25:34

The following verse in the book of Ephesians expands our understanding that, early on, His heart was for us to become His sons and daughters through adoption:

He chose us in Him before the foundation of the world, that we would be holy and blameless before Him. In love He predestined us to adoption as sons through Jesus Christ to Himself, according to the kind intention of His will, to the praise of the glory of His grace, which He freely bestowed on us in the Beloved.

~ Ephesians 1:4-6

In the first few passages of Ephesians 2, we read about the work of the cross to bring the Jewish nation and all other nations together as one.

Therefore, remember that formerly you, the Gentiles [all other nations] in the flesh ... were at that time separate from Christ ... and strangers to the covenants of promise, having no hope and without God in the world.

But now in Christ Jesus you who formerly were far off have been brought near by the blood of Christ. For He Himself is our peace, who made both groups into one [Jews and Gentiles] and broke down the barrier of the dividing wall, by abolishing in His flesh the enmity, [jealousy brought about by the Torah] ... so that in Himself He might make the two into one new man, thus establishing peace, and might reconcile them both in one body to God through the cross, by it having put to death the enmity.

~ Ephesians 2:11-16

Before we leave this topic, allow me to shed some light on the meaning of the enmity Jesus put to death:

By abolishing in His [own crucified] flesh the enmity [caused by] the Law with its decrees and ordinances [which He annulled]; that He from the two might create in Himself one new man [one new quality of humanity out of the two], so making peace.

~ Ephesians 2:15, AMPC

This is a Scripture often used to teach that we are no longer under the Law. A better explanation is that we who have accepted

Jesus as our Savior, both Jew, and Gentile, are no longer under the *penalty* of the Law.

Jesus addresses this misunderstanding in Matthew. I have found the *Power New Testament*[1] to be the best translation to make clear Jesus' response to this issue:

> *"Do not think that I came to annul, to bring an incorrect interpretation to the Torah or the Prophets: I did not come to annul but to bring spiritual abundance, for the Torah to be obeyed as it should be and God's promises to receive fulfillment. For truly I say to you: until the sky and the Earth would pass away, not one yod or one vav could ever pass away from the Torah, until everything would come to pass."*

> ~ Matthew 5:17-18, PNT

A New Covenant

In Jeremiah 31, God declares that He is going to give Israel a New Covenant—a covenant where He will write the Law on their hearts. The fullness of that covenant is His promise that they will know Him. The seal of all biblical covenants is the shedding of blood. This New Covenant is available as a result of Jesus' shed blood, His sacrifice for us on the cross. This covenant is extended first to the Jewish people and then to the nations, the Gentiles. This covenant not only assures us of eternal life but also creates the pathway that results in the forming of a new humanity—the One New Man of Ephesians 2.

> *"Behold, days are coming," declares the LORD, "when I will make a new covenant with the house of Israel and with the house of Judah, not like the covenant which I made with their*

---

[1] William J. Morford, translator. The Power New Testament: Revealing Jewish Roots, 4th ed. (Travelers Rest, SC: True Potential Publishing, Inc., 2007)

fathers in the day I took them by the hand to bring them out of the land of Egypt, My covenant which they broke, although I was a husband to them," declares the LORD.

"But this is the covenant which I will make with the house of Israel after those days," declares the LORD, "I will put My law within them and on their heart I will write it; and I will be their God, and they shall be My people. They will not teach again, each man his neighbor and each man his brother, saying, 'Know the LORD,' for they will all know Me, from the least of them to the greatest of them," declares the LORD, "for I will forgive their iniquity, and their sin I will remember no more."

~ Jeremiah 31:31-34

Perhaps, in this passage, it is best to use the true Hebrew definition of the word *law*, which is "instructions." Yeshua/Jesus did not annul the Torah, or the Law, as many have taught. He annulled the *enmity*. The enmity was the jealousy from the pride of the Jews about the Torah and the ignorance of the Gentiles concerning the Torah.

David Stern defined *enmity* in these words: "Mutual dislike of each other's customs [practices, author insert]. This is a common cause of friction between cultures, but in this instance, Jewish customs are different for a unique reason. They did not merely evolve; rather, they were the Jewish people's response to the Torah… This is why it is appropriate to say that the enmity between Jews and Gentiles was occasioned by the *Torah*."[2]

If the Ephesians passage is studied in the Greek, you will see that, in the definitions for *law*, with its decrees and ordinances, Paul is referring to the *oral laws* that separated the Jews from the Gentiles, calling them "unclean." This brings to mind Acts 10, where the Lord shows Peter in a dream not to call unclean what He calls clean.

---

[2] Stern, David H., *Jewish New Testament Commentary: A Companion Volume to the Jewish New Testament* (Cedar Rapids, IA: Jewish New Testament Publishers, 1992), p. 585.

That statement was in no way referring to food. It was about the incorrect concept that Gentiles who received Messiah were still considered "unclean."

I have come to understand that it was aspects of the oral Torah, not the written Torah, that laid the foundation for a strict separation between Jew and non-Jew. The Torah and the prophets give a clear instruction against erecting barriers to separate Israel from the nations. The foreigner who desires to worship the God of Abraham, Isaac, and Jacob was to be welcomed into the community and treated with the same respect as the native-born. The foreigner was to be offered full participation in matters of Torah and Torah life. The prophets pronounced judgment upon any who would neglect their God-given responsibility to the stranger on the same grounds as the neglect of orphans and widows.

Now God did say for His people to "come out from among them"—the pagan people—so as not to stray from the ways of the God of Abraham, Isaac, and Jacob. However, that did not apply to those who chose to honor the ways of the God that the Jewish people served.

At the end of the chapter, we discover the reason for this merging: God wants to create a dwelling place where He can be with all His family.

In the following Scripture, Paul is bringing further clarity to God's heart for the Gentiles:

> *The Scripture, foreseeing that God would justify the Gentiles by faith, preached the gospel beforehand to Abraham, saying, "ALL THE NATIONS WILL BE BLESSED IN YOU." So then those who are of faith are blessed with Abraham, the believer.*
>
> Galatians 3:8-9

Abraham is referred to in the New Testament with the promise to the Gentiles. The opening words "The Scripture" in the above passage is alluding to Genesis 12, as the New Testament had not been written in Abraham's time.

For many years, before I came to understand the role of being a Jew in the Body of Christ, people would come up to me and say something like this: "How wonderful that you are a Jewish believer!"

In response, I would quickly quote the following Scripture:

> *There is neither Jew nor Greek, there is neither slave nor free man, there is neither male nor female; for you are all one in Christ Jesus. And if you belong to Christ, then you are Abraham's descendants, heirs according to promise.*
>
> Galatians 3:28-29

"See?" I would say with a shrug of my shoulders. "We are all one. No big deal."

Then God got ahold of me one day and asked, *Do I still create men and women?*

"Yes, of course, Lord," I replied.

Then, Joan, find out what that Scripture is really saying.

God is still creating males and females, Jews and "Greeks" (representing all Gentile believers in this context). Paul was showing the Gentile believers in that day that their natural differences did not separate them from oneness in the Spirit. Through the centuries, the Jewish people, against all odds, remain. This validates God's faithfulness to His promises in His Word. The very existence of the Jewish people today is our surety that His Word is eternal.

Yet, Gentile children adopted into God's family by faith are also Abraham's descendants. They can believe that all His faithful promises to their brother Israel remain true. The ancient picture book of God's Word reveals that He retains that promise to the foundational people of the Commonwealth of Israel forever, no matter how they stray. He demonstrates His unconditional love for ALL His children in this way. There were consequences for their disobedience, as we also experience, but His love never ceases.

However, be sure you understand that there is only *one way* to the Father for both Jews and Gentiles, and that is through His Son. That is why Paul writes to the Roman church in these words:

> *Brethren, my heart's desire and my prayer to God for them [the Jewish people] is for their salvation. For I testify about them that they have a zeal for God, but not in accordance with knowledge. For not knowing about God's righteousness and seeking to establish their own, they did not subject themselves to the righteousness of God.*
>
> *How then will they call on Him in whom they have not believed? How will they believe in Him whom they have not heard? And how will they hear without a preacher? How will they preach unless they are sent? Just as it is written, "HOW BEAUTIFUL ARE THE FEET OF THOSE WHO BRING GOOD NEWS OF GOOD THINGS!"*
>
> ~ Romans 10:1-3, 14-15

Dear Reader, it is harvest time, perhaps the *final* harvest. It is time to venture into the fields with the good news. The Plan is best expressed in this verse in Romans, telling us that God and all creation are yearning for the fellowship of believing Jews and Gentiles in unity providing God's ultimate dwelling place on earth.

> *"For the earnest expectation of the creation eagerly waits for the revealing of the sons of God"*
>
> ~ Romans 8:19, NKJV

Therefore remember that formerly you,
the Gentiles in the flesh, …. were at
that time separate from Christ, excluded
from the commonwealth of Israel, and
strangers to the covenants of promise,
having no hope and without
God in the world.

~ Ephesians 2:11a, 12

3

THE
COMMONWEALTH
OF ISRAEL

D O YOU FIND IT interesting that chapter two of
Ephesians makes a clear distinction that separation from
Christ also means *separation* from the commonwealth
of Israel and all its privileges? That separation includes the loss of
the *legal* right of citizenship. Without that citizenship the covenants
of promise do not apply. This scripture now brings clarity that the
work of the cross is not only unto salvation but unto positioning as
a citizen of the commonwealth of Israel. God is showing us in His
plan that He wants all nations to be joined to the foundational work
He laid out when He created Israel as His pattern for community.

*[Remember] that you were at that time separated (living apart)
from Christ [excluded from all part in Him], utterly estranged*

and outlawed from the rights of Israel as a nation, and strangers with no share in the sacred compacts of the [Messianic] promise [with no knowledge of or right in God's agreements, His covenants]. And you had no hope (no promise); you were in the world without God.

~ Ephesians 2:12, AMPC

Going one step further the following Scripture also found in Ephesians 2 reveals how I came to believe that the term *commonwealth* refers to God's dwelling place.

Through him you Gentiles are also joined together as part of this dwelling where God lives by his Spirit.

~ Ephesians 2:22, NLT

In Him [and in fellowship with one another] you yourselves also are being built up [into this structure] with the rest, to form a fixed abode (dwelling place) of God in (by, through) the Spirit.

~ Ephesians 2:22, AMPC

The above Scriptures (in different translations) point clearly to the fact that those who believe in the work of the cross, whether Jew or Gentile, have all the privileges of being part of God's Commonwealth of Israel. Also, these Scriptures bring clarity to the fact that believing Jews and Gentiles coming together, by the Spirit, create a dwelling place for God on Earth.

By learning the definition of commonwealth, God showed me that it was the initial model of His Kingdom on Earth revealed through the story of the Israelites.

Let me take you on my path of discovery with the Merriam-Webster dictionary. The dictionary tells us: A commonwealth is "founded on law and united by compact or tacit agreement of the people for the common good."[1]

Commonwealth in *Strong's Concordance* in Ephesians 2:11-12 is the number G4174, *politeia*; from G4176, which is translated "citizenship."[2]

The word in this verse is G1429, *dodekaphulon*, translated from the Greek as "the twelve tribes" from the words *dodeka* and *phule*, "commonwealth of Israel," which is mentioned only once in the Bible.[3] Israel, as a nation, was founded at Mount Sinai by God through the Laws given to Moses. These Laws, the Ten Commandments, are often called Israel's constitution.

A modern definition of the word *constitution* is a document to provide a permanent framework of the government to form a more perfect union to establish justice and ensure peace of the nation. The God-given instruction or law to Moses fits that definition, along with providing guidelines of relationship with God and with each other.

From day one, the biblical accounts show us God was communicating His ways to His people. It does not take long to discover that following instructions was not something they did well. Almost everything Moses recorded at the mountain had been spoken directly by God to many individuals before the Israelites ever reached Mount Sinai.

Sabbath was the first thing He instituted on the seventh day of creation. Observing the Sabbath was the first serious test He gave Israel before they reached Sinai.

---

[1] Both translations make it very clear the work of the cross in providing a legal right of citizenship to the Commonwealth of Israel.

[2] Strong's Concordance of the Bible, s.v. "commonwealth."

[3] Strong's Concordance of the Bible, s.v. "the twelve tribes."

Instruction on sacrifice was given to Cain and Able (see Hebrews 11:4). We read that Noah knew which animals God considered "clean" to offer for sacrifice:

> *"You shall take with you of every clean animal by sevens, a male and his female; and of the animals that are not clean two, a male and his female.*

> ~ Genesis 7:2

Perhaps, God thought, *if I write my instructions in stone, they might just have a better understanding of the importance of obeying Me. At least they can't ignore it.*

God's instructions became a written covenant giving the tribes their unity, a common and foundational way of functioning on principles acceptable to Him. They also had a common bloodline through Abraham. Yet there was diversity in the tribes, each one with its own identity, individuality, and uniqueness of purpose or calling.

Remembering that God was showing us a model of His heart and ways, He continues that model today. His creation is diverse with many nations and tongues. Nations, as well as each of us, are created with a destiny that no one else could fulfill—the purpose of establishing His Kingdom on Earth as it is in heaven.

The Oneness of Believers

In the year 2020, oneness and unity were highlighted through many prophetic voices as we prayed…for the destiny of the global Body of Yeshua/Jesus. Until now, I had thought unity and oneness were interchangeable. However, through the teachings of Clay Nash, now I understand with greater impact Yeshua's/Jesus' words in John 17 that we would be one as He and the Father are one.

Unity is defined as "the state of being united or joined as a whole or the state of different areas or groups being joined together to form a single country or organization." Now I also understand unity is the process. In unity, people assemble in that common process.

God shows us His process in the picture book of Israel that was initially a nation with twelve tribes conquering Canaan by obedience to God's direction … until pride and disobedience became a dividing factor. Unity is His means of how He would eventually bring us to oneness. Clay Nash states that unity releases temporary momentum, oneness creates a synergy that maximizes purpose.

When we look at that model of Israel, we can see the individuality of the twelve tribes. God set their boundaries and divine purposes. He set their positions around the tabernacle of His presence and their place in His army for war. They had their own banners and characteristics. Today, God sets us in place according to His design of our destiny. The following Scripture shows us His heart:

> *He made from one man every nation of mankind to live on all the face of the earth, having determined their appointed times and the boundaries of their habitation.*
>
> ~ Acts 17:26

Oneness, according to Clay Nash, is the product of the process.[4] Oneness is how we should finish. I believe oneness is the gift Yeshua/Jesus prayed for and gave to us by shedding His blood at Calvary. Until then, mankind could only have unity through covenant. Relationship with God was based on man entering into covenant with God by following His instructions and receiving redemption through multiple sacrifices and intervention through intercession by the Levites (priests).

4 Clay Nash Ministries, www.claynash.org.

At the Passover table, Yeshua/Jesus made it clear when He held up the cup and said to His disciples, this cup is the New Covenant in My blood" (1 Corinthians 11:25), referring to Jeremiah's words:

> *"But this is the covenant which I will make with the house of Israel after those days," says the LORD: "I will put My law in their minds, and write it on their hearts; and I will be their God, and they shall be My people. No more shall every man teach his neighbor, and every man his brother, saying, 'Know the LORD,' for they all shall know Me, from the least of them to the greatest of them, says the LORD. For I will forgive their iniquity, and their sin I will remember no more."*
>
> ~ Jeremiah 31:33-34

Once He was crucified and resurrected, the pathway was open for those who would acknowledge His life as a sacrifice for their sins. They could be one with the Father as Yeshua/Jesus was one with the Father. They could also be one with their brothers and sisters in Christ who chose that relationship and entered into the household of God. With the outpouring of the Holy Spirit, the Law or instructions of God would be written on their hearts and they would know Him personally.

In Ephesians 2, Paul explains that God was drawing all believers into the Commonwealth of Israel, which are the twelve tribes, according to the definition above. From this foundational picture, God would bring together His sons and daughters, according to His covenantal love laid out in His Word. At the end of this chapter in Paul's letter to the Ephesians, it becomes clear that this Commonwealth of believers would become God's dwelling place.

God's picture shows a blueprint of His end-time plan that, even in the diversity of the many nations, He would bring forth at the end of time as we know it. People from *all* of those nations, people of every tongue, and every tribe will worship Him together.

*And they sang a new song, saying, "Worthy are You to take the
book and to break its seals; for You were slain, and purchased
for God with Your blood men from every tribe and tongue and
people and nation. You have made them to be a kingdom and
priests to our God; and they will reign upon the earth."*

~ Revelation 5:9-10

With all their individuality, what made the twelve tribes the
Commonwealth of Israel was, first, the human bloodline connection
through Abraham. Now, all believers have a bloodline connection
through Yeshua/Jesus as adopted sons and daughters.

Second, through Abraham, God cut a covenant connection with
them that continued as a nation at Mount Sinai. He then carried
it into a New Covenant, expressed to Israel in Jeremiah 31, and
fulfilled that with Yeshua's/Jesus' blood. That blood gave Gentiles
access to the Commonwealth and the ability to become partakers of
all the covenantal promises.

Consider this: the nations of whom Abraham will become
the father are the very nations that God will call to be part of
the Commonwealth of Israel as found in Ephesians and again in
Galatians.

*The Scripture, foreseeing that God would justify the Gentiles by
faith, preached the gospel beforehand to Abraham, saying, "ALL
THE NATIONS WILL BE BLESSED IN YOU." So then those who
are of faith are blessed with Abraham, the believer.*

~ Galatians 3:8-9

Take note that "the Scripture" quoted in this verse refers to the
Old Testament. The New Testament was not yet written.

The Restoration

What more do we need to know about ourselves as one new humanity, One New Man? We were both (the Jewish people and all the nations of the world) created to be the dwelling place of God. How awesome! We are to be the restoration of what was lost in the Garden; a dwelling place where God can have fellowship with man.

Yeshua/Jesus stated He only came to the lost sheep of the House of Israel (see Matthew 15:24). He also sent the original followers only to the House of Israel (see Matthew 10:6). Why? Because they were to be the carriers of His Word and were called to be a light to the nations. They were the people of The Plan and they still are—both those who believe in Yeshua/Jesus and those who do not.

Romans 11:29 makes it very clear that their call is irrevocable. The word *their* refers to all Jewish people and as we, the believing Ekklesia, enter into our role, we will see the fullness of God's plan. God, in His ultimate wisdom, has given us a level playing field; He is not a God of partiality. As we see in Scripture from the beginning, He desires that *all* come to salvation through His Son.

In the book of Revelation, it is clear that Yeshua/Jesus, the Lamb of God, was slain for the nations. Here is a sidebar. You see the words, *"and they will reign upon the earth"* (Revelation 5:10).

Family of God, Heaven is *not* our destiny. Ruling and reigning on planet Earth is our destiny! This destiny will come to pass when Yeshua/Jesus sits upon the throne of David in Jerusalem.

Let's look once again at the following verse in Ephesians.

> *...remember that you (Gentiles) were at that time separate from Christ, excluded from the commonwealth of Israel, and strangers to the covenants of promise, having no hope and without God in the world.*

> ~ Ephesians 2:12

This verse clearly states the importance of the work of the cross as the means to be part of the Commonwealth of Israel. Yet the Church, for the most part, today, has separated itself from that Commonwealth. They have concentrated on the fact that the blood of Yeshua/Jesus, having paid the price of the penalty for sin, gives us access to the Father. This is an extremely important truth; for without that blood, we have no fellowship with Father God. However, here in Ephesians, the blood is stated as the means to bring Gentiles into the Commonwealth of Israel.

Let me be clear: I am not saying that everyone who is adopted into the household of faith should take on what we know as Jewish ways. What I believe is that God intended for us to keep the model that He gave the Israelites as a means of revealing His ways to us. However, that model has been so modified by man's tradition that only through the Holy Spirit's revelation and impartation can we, as the One New Man, walk according to the true heart of God.

But now in Christ Jesus you who formerly were far off have been brought near by the blood of Christ. For He Himself is our peace, who made both groups into one and broke down the barrier of the dividing wall.

~ Ephesians 2:13-14

Do you see it? Both groups! The Jewish people and the Gentiles together. The work of the cross (the redemption for the world) was the instrument to bring The Plan of the One New Man to planet Earth. God started to reveal this with the Hebrews and continued at the cross to explain this plan for world redemption. However, the full strategies of this mystery were yet to unfold.

The Beginning of the Ekklesia

Here is another thought to ponder about the foundation God laid for the Ekklesia or the Commonwealth. When God enlarged His plan to establish Israel as a nation, He saw it was time to document the structure by which the Commonwealth should live. Thus, the recording of this constitution was given to Moses on Mount Sinai.

The structure of this relationship, called the covenant, was sealed with blood. This foreshadowed the eternal covenant, which would be sealed once and for all by the matchless blood of Yeshua/Jesus.

May I suggest that the Ekklesia began at that time? God laid the foundation of the covenant, of which *all* believers would become part, through the precious shed blood of the cross. Even at that time, there was a mixed multitude that came out of Egypt. This mixed multitude, for the most part, were those who chose to serve the one God they found to be reliable. They were attaching themselves to the Israelites by faith.

> *This is the one (Moses) who was in the congregation in the wilderness together with the angel who was speaking to him on Mount Sinai, and who was with our fathers; and he received living oracles to pass on to you.*
>
> ~ Acts 7:38

If you look up the word *congregation in Strong's Concordance,* it reads: G*1577*. ekklēsia; from G*1537* and G*2564*; *an assembly,* a (religious) *congregation:*—assembly.[5]

Accepting that Mount Sinai was God's foundation for the Ekklesia, one can see that God gave to the Israelites His instructions for governing and living as a community and the responsibilities (activities) of the priesthood. The Levitical priesthood was a type and shadow for us. When Yeshua/Jesus became the final sacrifice,

---

[5] Strong's Concordance of the Bible, s.v. "ekkelsia."

the shadow now had substance. When Yeshua/Jesus ascended to Heaven and stepped into His role as the Melchizedek priest, we, in Christ, also became part of the Melchizedek priesthood.

The Melchizedek Priesthood

And Melchizedek king of Salem brought out bread and wine; now he was a priest of God Most High.

~ Genesis 14:18

This Scripture introduces us to Melchizedek as a king and a priest. This is highly unusual, for in biblical times you could not be both. The following Scriptures tell us more about this somewhat mysterious person. Hebrews continues to shed light on this Melchizedek as Yeshua/Jesus Himself before His actual birth on Earth. For us who are in Christ, it shows we are not only priests to intercede but also of the royal lineage to legislate God's will on Earth as it is in Heaven.

For this Melchizedek, king of Salem, priest of the Most High God, who met Abraham as he was returning from the slaughter of the kings and blessed him, to whom also Abraham apportioned a tenth part of all the spoils, was first of all, by the translation of his name, king of righteousness, and then also king of Salem, which is king of peace. Without father, without mother, without genealogy, having neither beginning of days nor end of life, but made like the Son of God, he remains a priest perpetually.

~ Hebrews 7:1-3

What Melchizedek did in Genesis was to serve the first covenant meal of bread and wine to Abraham. I believe in that moment Abraham met his Messiah. Thus, we read in John:

"Your father Abraham rejoiced to see My day, and he saw it and was glad." So the Jews said to Him, "You are not yet fifty years old, and have You seen Abraham?" Jesus said to them, "Truly, truly, I say to you, before Abraham was born, I am." Therefore they picked up stones to throw at Him, but Jesus hid Himself and went out of the temple.

~ John 8:56-59

In Hebrews, we can also read about Melchizedek. Yeshua/Jesus reminds us of the last covenant meal He served the disciples. He made it clear that He was the fellowship offering and the only way to the Father as they received the understanding of His body and His blood.

In the days of His flesh, He offered up both prayers and supplications with loud crying and tears to the One able to save Him from death, and He was heard because of His piety. Although He was a Son, He learned obedience from the things which He suffered. And having been made perfect, He became to all those who obey Him the source of eternal salvation, being designated by God as a high priest according to the order of Melchizedek.

~ Hebrews 5:7-10

And so my covenant brothers and sisters who are now the Commonwealth of Israel; through the blood of Yeshua/Jesus, Paul tells us in Revelation that unto God we are kings and priests.

And hast made us unto our God kings and priests: and we shall reign on the earth.

~ Revelation 5:10, KJV

Because you are sons, God has sent forth
the Spirit of His Son into our hearts,
crying, "Abba! Father!"

~ Galatians 4:6

4

SONSHIP

The Members of the Commonwealth—
the Sons and Daughters

S ONSHIP AND ADOPTION ARE very important to the
Father. He calls Israel, "My Son, My firstborn" (Exodus
4:22). He gave His only Son, Yeshua/Jesus, to redeem the
world and make a way for all to be adopted into His household. Our
acceptance of Yeshua/Jesus gives us the right to call God *Abba*, the
Hebrew word for "Daddy."

In the book of Exodus, He instructs Moses to tell the Israelites:

"Now then, if you will indeed obey My voice and keep My
covenant, then you shall be My own possession among all the
peoples, for all the earth is Mine; and you shall be to Me a
kingdom of priests and a holy nation.' These are the words that
you shall speak to the sons of Israel."

~ Exodus 19:5-6

Remember, we are looking at the picture of the model for *all* who love the Lord. A key phrase in the passage above is "the sons of Israel."

In 1 Peter, we are revisiting the promise of His love for the Israelites, desiring them to be a holy people with whom the nations (Gentiles) will become one through the blood of Yeshua/Jesus. In Peter, the fuller picture is presented to the Gentile believers (adopted children) who are now, according to Ephesians 2, citizens of the Commonwealth of Israel:

> *But you are A CHOSEN PEOPLE, A ROYAL PRIESTHOOD, A HOLY NATION, A PEOPLE FOR GOD'S OWN POSSESSION, so that you may proclaim the excellencies of Him who has called you out of darkness into His marvelous light.*
>
> ~ 1 Peter 2:9

I also believe an important prophetic picture can be found in Genesis when Jacob prays for Joseph's sons who were born in Egypt of a Gentile mother. Let's look now at this passage as a revelation of sonship.

> *And now your two sons, [Ephraim and Manasseh], who were born to you in the land of Egypt before I came to you in Egypt, are mine. [I am adopting them, and now] as Reuben and Simeon, [they] shall be mine.*
>
> ~ Genesis 48:5, AMPC

Jacob, the father of Joseph, pronouncing that Joseph's sons shall be viewed the same as Reuben and Simeon, is a prophetic picture bequeathing equal sonship to the Gentiles who would come to honor the God of Abraham, Isaac, and Jacob ... and eventually His Son, Yeshua/Jesus. They would have the same right of the firstborn along with the firstborn sons of the twelve tribes of Israel. They would not replace Reuben and Simeon as firstborn sons but would come alongside, adopted into the household with full privileges of the firstborn. This is also a clear revelation of the heart of our God for Sonship.

> *Therefore you are no longer outsiders (exiles, migrants and aliens, excluded from the rights of citizens), but you now share citizenship with the saints (God's own people, consecrated and set apart for Himself); and you belong to God's [own].*

> ~ Ephesians 2:19, AMPC

When one is adopted into a family, the father of the home sets the family values for all to follow. The adopted individual does not lose the identity of their country of origin but is expected to respect and follow the rules and values of the new permanent family. Gentiles are not asked to become Jews. Each has a role that is clearly stated in Romans 11. These roles in the One New Man are addressed in chapter 7 entitled *Level Playing Field*.

Sonship is how God as Father teaches His adopted sons and daughters His values. He teaches us from His Word. He longs for His adopted children to understand His heart of relationship now that they are part of His household.

God's "House Rules"

Once Israel became a nation, God began to reveal His house rules. Through the instructions He gave Moses He made it clear how His sons and daughters were to relate to Him and to each other. He also gave them His plan to follow His calendar which highlighted appointed times for them to gather and celebrate. These celebrations are times to reflect on His historic relationship with the Jewish people. They are times to interact with His Holy Spirit today and receive fresh revelation of His will and His ways. They are also "rehearsals" of celebrations that will continue in our future and in the future of the world.

Biblical study will show that keeping His calendar and His celebrations are for all His children now and in the future. These special occasions were initially given to the Jewish people to model God for us, but the Bible clearly calls them the Feasts of the Lord, not Jewish feasts.

Here are the statements of His heart to His adopted children:

For you have not received a spirit of slavery leading to fear again, but you have received a spirit of adoption as sons by which we cry out, "Abba! Father!"

~ Romans 8:15

So also we, while we were children, were held in bondage under the elemental things of the world. But when the fullness of the time came, God sent forth His Son, born of a woman, born under the Law, so that He might redeem those who were under the Law, that we might receive the adoption as sons. Because you are sons, God has sent forth the Spirit of His Son into our hearts, crying, "Abba! Father!" Therefore you are no longer a slave, but a son; and if a son, then an heir through God.

~ Galatians 4:3-7

In Romans 9:4-5 Paul speaks of the Jewish people, who are the Israelites. To them belong the adoption as sons, the glory and the covenants, the giving of the Law, the temple service, and the promises.

Let's look at God's picture book again. We see the Israelites are considered adopted by the faith of Abraham, who believed God. Yet Romans 11 also tells us they were broken off because of *un*belief, although they still have an opportunity to return by faith in Messiah.

God also warns the Gentiles that they, too, could be broken off by unbelief.

In Galatians 4, we see the Gentiles also are adopted by faith in Messiah. Clearly, both the Jewish people and the Gentiles are brought into the family by adoption through faith.

The Church has taken Scriptures and isolated them, based on the fact that according to Ephesians 2, the right to call Him "Father/Abba" comes from Yeshua's/Jesus' work on the cross. True, but the cross also gives one the right to join the Commonwealth of His firstborn, Israel.

That does not mean that adopted sons and daughters become Jewish. No matter from which nation one originated, one is still adopted only by accepting the work of the cross. Thereby, they receive, through faith, the right of adoption into the household of God. All Abba's children have not only an individual identity as Abba's children but also membership with full rights and privileges to the Father's household; the household founded by the Lord through the twelve tribes of Jacob (the Commonwealth of Israel). Should we not then honor what God began—this plan of which we have become a part?

Face to Face with God

When God originally laid the foundation of His house as the structure of what He planned for His family, He talked face to face with the first humans He created. Adam and Eve had sweet fellowship with the Father until the Fall when this direct interaction began to be less frequent.

I have suggested within the pages of this book that the Father must have given instructions to Adam and Eve as parents, explaining the concept of the necessity of approaching the Father through sacrifice to continue fellowship with Him. Surely, Enoch understood

His ways as well; so much so that God took him up supernaturally to dwell with Him (Genesis 5:21-24). Perhaps Enoch taught the ways of God to his great-grandson Noah, and that was how Noah knew which animals were considered clean to be taken into the ark for the purpose of sacrifice.

Abram, who became Abraham, had face-to-face encounters with God. These he taught to his children. These lessons were passed on generationally by oral instruction and example.

Throughout the Old Testament, the revelation of God's Son was presented in such a way that, as The Plan unfolded, those that knew the Torah would not miss the appearing of their Messiah.

In the New Testament, Paul made that clear when he said to Timothy:

> *You, however, continue in the things you have learned and become convinced of, knowing from whom you have learned them, and that from childhood you have known the sacred writings which are able to give you the wisdom that leads to salvation through faith which is in Christ Jesus. All Scripture is inspired by God and profitable for teaching, for reproof, for correction, for training in righteousness; so that the man of God may be adequate, equipped for every good work.*
>
> ~ 2 Timothy 3:14-17

Keep in mind when Paul refers to "sacred writings" and "all Scripture" in the passage above, he is referring to the Old Testament for the New Testament was not yet written.

As God made sure the evidence of Yeshua/Jesus was available for His firstborn, He also made sure that Paul understood that the revelation of His Son was to be given to the Gentiles at the time of Yeshua's/Jesus' appearance.

In Ephesians 3, there is a piece that has been missed by most believers. The following verses point to the importance of the body receiving this revelation:

> *For this reason I, Paul, the prisoner of Christ Jesus for the sake of you Gentiles—if indeed you have heard of the stewardship of God's grace which was given to me for you; that by revelation there was made known to me the mystery, as I wrote before in brief. By referring to this, when you read you can understand my insight into the mystery of Christ, which in other generations was not made known to the sons of men, as it has now been revealed to His holy apostles and prophets in the Spirit; to be specific, that the Gentiles are fellow heirs and fellow members of the body, and fellow partakers of the promise in Christ Jesus through the gospel, of which I was made a minister, according to the gift of God's grace which was given to me according to the working of His power. To me, the very least of all saints, this grace was given, to preach to the Gentiles the unfathomable riches of Christ, and to bring to light what is the administration of the mystery which for ages has been hidden in God who created all things; so that the manifold wisdom of God might now be made known through the church to the rulers and the authorities in the heavenly places. This was in accordance with the eternal purpose which He carried out in Christ Jesus our Lord, in whom we have boldness and confident access through faith in Him.*
>
> ~ Ephesians 3:1-12

It is again emphasized in Colossians:

> *Of this church [the Gentile church Paul was called to] I was made a minister according to the stewardship from God bestowed on me for your (the Gentiles) benefit, so that I might fully carry out the preaching of the word of God that is, the mystery [which was that Gentiles would be part of God's eternal*

plan of salvation] which has been hidden from the past ages and generations, [Originally God only brought His ways to the Hebrews/Israelites because they were chosen to be a people to reveal God's heart, His ways and His Son. The mystery was that it was His way of showing the world that He loved the world and was going to send Jesus through the Jewish bloodline.] but has now been manifested to His saints, to whom God willed to make known what is the riches of the glory of this mystery among the Gentiles, which is Christ in you, the hope of glory.

~ Colossians 1:25-27

What is the Church making known to the angelic rulers and demonic principalities? That God's eternal purpose was that none would be lost. Jews and Gentiles through Yeshua/Jesus would be the sons and daughters of God.

May we embrace that the One New Man is the end-game strategy God has presented in His Word to usher in the second coming of His Son! It is the key to bring about world revival and is only possible by oneness. The result will be the following:

I do not ask on behalf of these alone, (the original disciples) but for those also who believe in Me through their word; that they may all be one; even as You, Father, are in Me and I in You, that they also may be in Us, so that the world may believe that You sent Me.

~ John 17:20-21

I cannot emphasize this point enough. The end goal of the One New Man is that we be one even as Yeshua/Jesus and the Father are one, so the world will know Yeshua/Jesus was sent by God for the redemption of the world.

So then you [Gentiles] are no longer strangers and aliens, but you are fellow citizens with the saints [Jews], and are of God's household, having been built on the foundation of the apostles and prophets, Christ Jesus Himself being the cornerstone.

~ Ephesians 2:19-20, AMP

5

FIRM FOUNDATION

G OD IS A GOD of order. Because of His nature, He
has graciously given us a blueprint of how He wants
to build His Ekklesia. God's Ekklesia is a structure of
living stones made up of those who have chosen to embrace the gift
of salvation, purchased for us through Christ Jesus. Thus, we are
members of God's household.

In His Word, God tells us that we, as the Ekklesia, must have a
firm foundation made up of apostles and prophets, with Christ Jesus
as the Cornerstone. In the following passage, He shows us that the
foundation stones are appointed by Him:

> *Now you are Christ's body, and individually members of it. And
> God has appointed in the church, first apostles, second prophets,
> third teachers.*

> ~ 1 Corinthians 12:27-28

I think the functions of apostles and prophets are often misunderstood. Many believers have formed their biblical picture of apostles and prophets based on Bible stories. Unfortunately, most have little knowledge of the roles of these leading figures, both those mentioned in the Word and those living today. An understanding of their giftings and purpose gives us the reason God considers them foundational building blocks of His Ekklesia.

The Apostle

When I think of the biblical stories of the apostles—the sent-out ones[1] who preached the Gospel—I focus on what they taught and how I can apply their lessons to my own life. I think about their journey—what they encountered, how they walked in supernatural power through the Holy Spirit, and how they often suffered for their faith. Their stories are both encouraging and sobering. I regard these early heroes as courageous individuals who were sent on a mission.

Yet, God was showing us so much more. Just as He did by letting us experience the stories of the Jewish people in the Old Testament, He is again giving us a model of His ways, His heart, and His Son through New Testament stories of the apostles' lives. Through their lives and ministry, God is showing us foundational truths of how He wants the Ekklesia to operate till His return. What we learn by example is a lesson for us personally, but we must expand our vision to understand that He is teaching us strategies for building His Kingdom on Earth as it is in Heaven.

In my fifty-plus years in the Body of Christ, it is only in the last decade that emphasis has been again put on the role of the apostle. Sadly, there are those in the Body of Christ who feel the office of the apostle ended with the early Church. Yet, here in Ephesians, we are shown the apostle's role is important as a foundation to build on.

---

[1] In *Strong's Concordance*, #G652, apostolos means "one sent forth from by another," Greek Bible Lexicon, www.Lexiconcordance.com, accessed Feb. 17, 2021.

Always keep in mind we are building a dwelling place in the Spirit for God on Earth as it is in Heaven. A dwelling place for Him from generation to generation.

The literal translation of the word *apostle* means "one sent with a message." It is my opinion that the word *apostle* should be understood to be a job description, not a title of hierarchy, with these "sent ones" lording it over others in a congregation. God gives specific giftings to those He appoints as apostles. The insights He gives them represent God's will as direction for the building of the Kingdom of God on Earth. Reading through the Gospels, you can see that definition rightly describes the twelve men that Jesus initially picked to share His teachings with the people of their day. The gift is to be honored and respected. They have an anointing to put things in order. A true apostle raises up other apostles, prophets, teachers, pastors, and evangelists to equip the members to minister.

That was the story of the early apostles as they traveled, sharing the Gospel and setting the Ekklesia in order in each town as evidenced by their writings.

Although he or she walks in authority given by God to present His blueprint, a true apostle will also have a mantle of humility. They are always open to accepting counsel from other members of the Body, especially prophets, to fulfill God's will. In other words, a true apostle will have a servant's heart as modeled by Yeshua/Jesus.

Calling them to Himself, Jesus said to them, "You know that those who are recognized as rulers of the Gentiles lord it over them; and their great men exercise authority over them. But it is not this way among you, but whoever wishes to become great among you shall be your servant; and whoever wishes to be first among you shall be slave of all. For even the Son of Man did not come to be served, but to serve, and to give His life a ransom for many."

~ Mark 10:42-45

Linda Heidler[2] gives us the following marks of a true apostle in the book, *The Apostolic Church Arising*.[3] The apostles' close relationship with Jesus makes them easily recognizable:

1. They have the ability to interpret what God is doing.

2. They are trustworthy with money.

3. They have the authority to discipline and pronounce judgment.

4. They lay down their lives for the Church.

5. They are "fathers and mothers" for the Church.

6. They have a revelation of Israel and the One New Man.

7. They stand in intercession for the Church.

8. They operate in the supernatural realm.

God sets high standards for those He anoints as apostles, but make no mistake, those standards should be ours as well. In this time of our history, discernment is key to our direction and protection. The necessity of being pure before the Lord guarantees our ability to hear clearly and navigate these perilous times. We also need apostolic and prophetic alignments in our life for direction, encouragement, and correction to keep us on course.

2 Linda Heidler is a prophetic intercessor and deliverance minister at Glory of Zion International Ministries.

3 Chuck Pierce and Robert Heidler, *The Apostolic Church Arising: God's People Gathering and Contending for the Glory Today* (Corinth, TX, Glory of Zion International Ministries, 2012)

The Prophet

Most of us are more familiar with the concept of a prophet from our Old Testament Bible stories than we are with the concept of an apostle from our New Testament stories. In some ways, the Old Testament prophets acted like apostles in giving direction and correction to Israel. They, too, often suffered for their service to the Lord in speaking truth to the hearers. The Old Testament prophets were set apart and often called on to execute prophetic acts as examples to the people. They operated in signs and wonders, healings and resurrections, and functioned as messengers of the Lord to the kings of their era.

For the most part, those who are called to the office of the prophet today live among us and are active on a national and local platform. They have been proven trustworthy, are held accountable by other prophetic voices, and usually operate with apostles. God has positioned prophets and apostles in every venue of life. We are now in a season when the Lord has led us outside the walls of the Church to meet the needs of the people. Marketplace ministry is similar to Jesus going to the hills to bring the Gospel to the people.

Anyone who has received Jesus as Savior and has been filled with His Holy Spirit can prophesy. That gift, however, does not put the person in the office of a prophet. The gift of prophecy is our ability to hear the Lord when we inquire of Him and then to share His heart.

Let's see what Paul has to say about prophecy:

Pursue love, yet desire earnestly spiritual gifts, but especially that you may prophesy. For one who speaks in a tongue does not speak to men but to God; for no one understands, but in his spirit he speaks mysteries. But one who prophesies speaks to men for edification and exhortation and consolation. One who speaks in a tongue edifies himself; but one who prophesies edifies the church. Now I wish that you all spoke in tongues, but even more

*that you would prophesy; and greater is one who prophesies
than one who speaks in tongues, unless he interprets, so that the
church may receive edifying.*

~ 1 Corinthians 14:1-5

It is clear Paul is encouraging all believers to seek the gift of
prophecy for the building of the Church. Many in the Body today
have been burned by false prophecy. Perhaps that is the result of
putting their trust more in individuals for direction than in seeking
the Lord for themselves. God's wisdom teaches us that every word
we receive should be tested and confirmed. It is important that the
character and accuracy of the prophet also be tested. That holds true
whether one has a large public platform or is simply someone within
your prayer group.

As young Timothy's mentor, Paul is telling him to take seriously
what was given him by trusted individuals in the Body of Christ at
that time.

*Do not neglect the spiritual gift within you, which was bestowed
on you through prophetic utterance with the laying on of hands
by the presbytery. Take pains with these things; be absorbed in
them, so that your progress will be evident to all.*

~ 1 Timothy 4:14-15

Paul encouraged Timothy to be diligent, to meditate, and to pray
over the prophetic words he received by the laying on of hands. In
that way, others will see how to hold on and prosper with the words
they receive.

When we receive a prophetic word from the Lord, our response
must be activated by our faith, our prayers, and sometimes a
prophetic action. In other words, receiving a prophetic word requires
our participation to see it come to pass.

We read in Daniel 9 and 10 that Daniel realized after reading a prophecy about Jerusalem, he had to fast and pray to establish God's Word on Earth.

Let me share an example from my own life of receiving a word from the Lord and walking in unbelief concerning it. Over twenty years ago, I was called out by a seasoned prophet in a church while visiting another country. The word was powerful, beyond what I had faith to believe. Instead of praying into it, I took an attitude of, *"Well, if it's God, it will happen."* Not a wise choice. I struggled for many years over that prophetic word until I finally repented and said, "Yes, Lord, I receive that word and trust You to work in me to perform Your will."

The prophetic word was about writing. I was told in that word, *"Write the books, write the manuals, train the end-time army."* I just did not have the confidence to answer that assignment. To take God at His word, I had to change my attitude. I had to decide to trust that He would give me what I needed to do what He was asking. Then I had to make a place in my day to write. Many people love writing; for me, it felt like a burden until I came into agreement with the Lord. This book is only one of several projects God has successfully produced through me. Obedience and action to cooperate with prophetic words are not always easy. Trust me, though, there is no other way.

Some denominations and individuals have decided to ignore the gift of prophecy, saying it is no longer operating in the world today. That, my friends, is serious, especially since God's Word tells us He gave us that gift to help us succeed (see 2 Chronicles 20:20).

In this new era, most prophets I have learned to respect are telling us that God is declaring He is going to do things with great acceleration. He is going to use the gifts many have put aside, taken for granted, or resisted. I certainly fell into the latter category.

I saw the gift of acceleration take place recently in a prayer gathering in my home. A gal in the baby-boomer generation, who had recently received the baptism of the Holy Spirit, began to reveal things she was seeing. She was incredibly accurate, and it was beautiful to see her gift come forth so early in her walk in the things of the Spirit.

God spoke and it was so. When we speak in agreement with God's Word, we bring about His will. I believe the gift of prophecy, along with the word of wisdom and the word of knowledge, are powerful tools to be used in evangelism and mentoring. They will assist us as we bring in and mature the harvest. However, those gifts are different from the anointing given to the one who is called by God to the office of the prophet.

Today's prophets establish revelatory gifts in the Body of Christ so that these gifts function as God intends. They are not just to prophesy but to set prophecy in order and establish an atmosphere where others can learn to prophesy. True prophets are those with great maturity and accuracy; when they speak, God backs them up. Their God-given words release a power that can change situations and empower the hearer to move more effectively in their calling and, eventually, to impart prophetic gifts to others.

In cooperation with the apostles, today's prophets are set in office to build the Kingdom of God and to bring the foundation of the five-fold ministry into proper order.

The brief descriptions I have given you of both the apostle and the prophet should show you why God has given them first place as foundational building blocks for His Kingdom. Both offices prepare us to be able to fulfill our calling. They work together to bring balance and maturity to the Body as we are sent to minister.

* * *

In the introduction of this book, I shared an encounter of the importance of aligning with the prophetic voice in this hour. Permit me now to share another part of that encounter I had with the Lord. It began with a phone call from a good friend and a full-time intercessor who was already engaged in some pretty heavy prayer assignments.

"Joanie," she said, "I need a midwife."

"How so?"

"I have been birthing something in the Spirit all day in intercession, and I need help to bring it forth."

Of course, I quickly agreed, and we began to pray on the phone. I can't explain the following in the natural; I can only relay what transpired in the next few moments. I was transported into the following vision:

I found myself in a hospital birthing room where four angels were assisting a birth. As we continued to pray, I saw that it was Donald J. Trump emerging from the birth canal. A gold crown was placed on his head. Having heard the prophecies that President Trump would fulfill a prophetic destiny according to Isaiah 45 as the 45th President of the United States—a type of King Cyrus—the crown made sense to me.

As I witnessed the birth and saw President Trump exit the birth canal, I heard the words: *"Can a nation be born in a day?"* I felt strongly the Lord was giving our nation a chance for new birth under President Trump's leadership.

The Isaiah 45 Scripture that speaks of King Cyrus has been applied today to President Trump by several respected prophetic voices. With our finite understanding, we often forget that God is outside of time and what He reveals in one generation can apply to other generations.

Case in point: Yeshua/Jesus was crucified before the foundation of the world. Generations later the redeeming work of the cross still applies today. It is a head-scratcher, for sure.

Scriptures instruct us that out of the mouth of two or three witnesses every word shall be established. That practice began in ancient times when two witnesses were required to validate the position of the new moon to verify that a new month was beginning. This practice kept the biblical calendar of the Lord accurate, so the Feasts of the Lord were celebrated at God's appointed times.

In the New Testament, we see that this practice has continued.

> *This is the third time I am coming to you. Every fact is to be confirmed by the testimony of two or three witnesses.*
>
> ~ 2 Corinthians 22:7

Of course, to take this to heart, you must believe that the prophetic is for today, or you could not accept it as a fact. I believe we, as the Body, must function obediently in our individual giftings. In that way, as we complement the diverse works of God in each other, we bring the whole counsel of God.

The Isaiah 45 Prophecy

King Cyrus was a devoted Zoroastrian, a member of an ancient Persian religion with many similarities to Judeo-Christian beliefs, such as one God, Heaven and Hell, and a day of judgment. It is recorded that King Cyrus ruled with the Zoroastrian law of *asha* (truth and righteousness), but he did not impose his belief system on those he conquered. He gave freedom to the Jews to return to Jerusalem from their captivity in Babylon. He even sent those who wanted to return to Jerusalem with provisions and the articles of worship that had been taken from the temple, so they could rebuild the temple according to the Word of the Lord.

Although Cyrus was faithful to his Zoroastrian beliefs, he had respect for the following Word of God in 2 Chronicles:

Now in the first year of Cyrus king of Persia—in order to fulfill the word of the LORD by the mouth of Jeremiah—the LORD stirred up the spirit of Cyrus king of Persia, so that he sent a proclamation throughout his kingdom, and also put it in writing, saying, "Thus says Cyrus king of Persia, 'The LORD, the God of heaven, has given me all the kingdoms of the earth, and He has appointed me to build Him a house in Jerusalem, which is in Judah. Whoever there is among you of all His people, may the LORD his God be with him, and let him go up!'"

~ 2 Chronicles 36:22-23

We have been told in God's Word that He does nothing without telling His prophets first.

Surely the Lord God does nothing unless He reveals His secret counsel to His servants the prophets.

~ Amos 3:7

The following Scripture about King Cyrus is proof positive as Isaiah prophesied this before King Cyrus was ever born.

"It is I who says of Cyrus, 'He is My shepherd! And he will perform all My desire.' And he declares of Jerusalem, 'She will be built,' And of the temple, 'Your foundation will be laid.'

"Thus says the LORD to Cyrus His anointed, whom I have taken by the right hand, to subdue nations before him and to loose the loins of kings; to open doors before him so that gates will not be shut: "I will go before you and make the rough places smooth; I will shatter the doors of bronze and cut through their iron bars. I will give you the treasures of darkness and hidden wealth of secret places, so that you may know that it is I, the LORD, the

God of Israel, who calls you by your name. For the sake of Jacob My servant, and Israel My chosen one, I have also called you by your name; I have given you a title of honor though you have not known Me.

"I am the LORD, and there is no other; besides Me there is no God. I will gird you, though you have not known Me; that men may know from the rising to the setting of the sun that there is no one besides Me. I am the LORD, and there is no other, the One forming light and creating darkness, causing well-being and creating calamity; I am the Lord who does all these."

~ Isaiah 44:28-45:1-7

The Trump Prophecy

Reading through the biblical and historical accounts of the Jewish people and King Cyrus, my eyes were open to the similarities we are facing today. King Cyrus, by the unction of Holy Spirit, was directed to help the Jewish people return and build the temple of the Lord. Keep in mind that King Cyrus was not a worshiper of the God of Israel, yet he had enough respect to honor God's direction.

Sadly, even though the king gave the Jews opportunity, provision, and the sacred temple vessels to help them to return and rebuild, only a remnant chose to return to their homeland. Many were happy to remain in the comfort of what they had built in captivity.

God states He anointed Cyrus to do a work for Him even though this pagan king did not know the Lord. The anointing given to Cyrus was the ability to deal with other nations, to open doors and gates of access to set things in order, not only for Israel but for other countries. God declares He will gird Cyrus with strength. President Trump indeed operated under that same anointing.

Today the Church is not much different from the Jewish people under King Cyrus's rule. During President Trump's leadership, we were given the same privilege to recover and rebuild. Yet, history repeats itself. Only a remnant of His people is willing to work and fight for the principles of God to rebuild His Kingdom in this generation.

Many are not even aware that we have been in captivity. Our privilege and position as believers have, by devious, anti-God design, been eroded and/or removed through legal and cultural pressures.

President Trump worked hard to provide an opportunity to reclaim our lost privileges. For example, to the Church in America, he gave back her voice by overturning the Johnson Amendment, which was a gag order placed on our pastors. He encouraged our leadership to speak out freely on the principles of the Kingdom concerning abortion, family values, and law and order. At the National Right to Life March in Washington, D.C., President Trump made a declaration that every child, born or unborn, was made in the image of God. As the God-appointed leader of our country, that statement had prophetic weight.

His work to put in conservative judges, across the land, and in the Supreme Court, is key to upholding our constitutional rights based on God's principles. This move is a generational move, put in place for our children and grandchildren. Our God is a generational God.

God's promise to King Cyrus has also played out in President Trump's interaction with the nations. He gained great respect from heads of state, as well as inciting a healthy fear in other countries. The strength he exhibited in dealing with the extreme difficulties and violent opposition encountered during his term has come from the Lord.

One of the most important spiritual steps President Trump took, by the unction of the Holy Spirit, was moving the US embassy back to Jerusalem. He was the first president to declare Jerusalem the true capital of Israel and follow through with action. That important act positioned America for the blessing of Genesis 12: "Those that bless you I will bless." Indeed, we have experienced a great deal of blessing regarding our economy, gaining worldwide respect under his leadership.

Yet, at the time of this writing, I believe that we are in the greatest testing of our generation concerning our faith in the prophetic words we have received for our nation. The story is not over yet. I have confidence we will yet see a turning to confirm the prophetic Word of the Lord that America will be saved!

As a member of the family of God, every believer needs to take seriously the fact that while President Trump was not at all perfect, he was, indeed chosen by God to put things in order in our country and internationally. Like Cyrus, God fashioned President Trump to put Israel in her proper place internationally. This has opened an opportunity for other nations to come into alignment with God's purpose concerning Israel as we enter the last of the last days.

* * *

In the writing of this section, the Lord brought to mind a vision I had a year ago. I thought I understood the vision at that time. Now I see it was more than a personal message. He was delivering a warning to us as His people to take heed and use discernment in this dangerous season.

When the vision opened, I found myself on a high and jagged mountain. My back was pressed into the mountain, and I was standing on a narrow ledge. There was a strong sense of danger as I became aware of the possibility that I could easily fall off the ledge. Looking down, I saw multitudes of people walking in the valley at the foot of the mountain. They appeared to be very small in size, simply because I was standing so high up on the mountain.

Single pages of a book were floating toward me, and I reached carefully to catch them, trying not to make any sudden movement that would cause me to slip. A black, shadowy figure approached, pressing me into the mountain. Initially, I was comforted, feeling safe in this precarious position.

Within a few seconds, however, I realized I was encountering a demonic entity and pushed it away. Immediately, I found myself in a flat area on top of the mountain, and I was *truly* safe. As I stood there, a white box came floating toward me. When I looked inside, I saw a thick book bound in white leather. I realized that some of the pages were those I had been trying to retrieve while on the side of the mountain. But the book contained considerably more pages, and I heard the voice of the Lord say, *"Lo, I come: in the volume of the book."* (see Psalm 40:7, KJV)

Through the words, *"Lo, I come: in the volume of the book,"* the Lord was showing me that when we receive only partial truth, it is a dangerous place to be. Satan will send bits and pieces of the truth, which can be misunderstood and provide false security. I was in a very risky position and, had I not discerned that the momentary comfort of partial truth was demonic, I would have remained there, unable to fulfill my calling to train the end-time army.

Partial truth can come to us from false biblical doctrine, the rewriting of our history, or through our current news media. The only safe place for us is in operating in the gift of discernment and receiving the whole counsel of the Lord.

When I questioned the Lord as to why He was showing me those individuals, He told me that they are the ones in the valley of decision. *No matter how far up the mountain of life they climb,* He said, *you must teach them they must be ever aware that their only hope of remaining on a solid footing is truth, the whole truth, and nothing but the truth.*

Navigating through life, our greatest asset is our ability to hear the heart of our heavenly Father. That is the gift of prophecy operating as we pray and the impartation of His Word as we study to show ourselves approved.

Call to Me and I will answer you, and I will tell you great and mighty things, which you do not know.

~ Jeremiah 33:3

Now, therefore, you are no longer
strangers and foreigners, but fellow
citizens with the saints and members of
the household of God...Jesus Himself
being the chief cornerstone.
~ Ephesians 2:19-20

6

YESHUA— CORNERSTONE OF THE FOUNDATION

B Y GOD'S DESIGN, THE Jewish people were not only to be the caretakers of the written Word, but also the natural bloodline of the Living Word, Yeshua/Jesus, the Word in flesh. So now let's take a look at the cornerstone from the Scriptures that reveal not only Yeshua's/Jesus' bloodline, but His intended purpose from the heart of God for us.

When I read this Scripture in Ephesians concerning the foundation of the household of God, my first thoughts were: *What is a cornerstone? What is its purpose?*

In architecture, the cornerstone is the first stone laid for a structure; all the other stones are laid in reference to this one. The cornerstone aligns or positions a building in a specific direction.

That certainly defines the work of Jesus. He is the starting and finishing point in the life of every believer.

I want to take a minute here to talk about alignment. If a building is to be strong and functional, it must be properly aligned. We, also, as the living stones of the structure for God's dwelling place, must have proper alignment with our brothers and sisters in Christ. It is necessary for us to have individuals in our lives that we trust to speak encouragement, correction, and direction into our lives. We are not meant to walk alone.

Yeshua/Jesus Himself was a picture of God's plan. Fully God and fully man—another head-scratcher—Yeshua's/Jesus' natural bloodline revealed Jewish and Gentile blood, yet He followed the model of worship and life as laid out in the Torah and the Prophets, given to the world to reveal God's heart. Jesus lived His life on Earth as a Hebrew (Jew) and He will return as one, too.

The Genealogy of Jesus

> *The record of the genealogy of Jesus the Messiah, the son of David, the son of Abraham: Abraham was the father of Isaac, Isaac the father of Jacob, and Jacob the father of Judah and his brothers. Judah was the father of Perez and Zerah by Tamar, Perez was the father of Hezron, and Hezron the father of Ram. Ram was the father of Amminadab, Amminadab the father of Nahshon, and Nahshon the father of Salmon. Salmon was the father of Boaz by Rahab, Boaz was the father of Obed by Ruth, and Obed the father of Jesse. Jesse was the father of David the king.*
>
> ~ Matthew 1:1-6

The Hebraic prophetic natural bloodline of Yeshua/Jesus is revealed (vv.1-5). This is to address the prophecies in the Old Testament that Messiah would come from the line of King David.

The One New Man's natural bloodline is revealed to us (v.5) where we see that Rahab, a Gentile woman, was the mother of Boaz and he was the father of Obed by Ruth, another Gentile woman. Perhaps having a Gentile mother prepared Boaz to accept Ruth, a Gentile, as his wife.

Yeshua's/Jesus' mixture of Gentile and Hebrew blood in the history of his natural line, while still living out His life according to the Scriptures, is a beautiful model God gave us of the One New Man.

In the following Scripture, Jesus unpacks the lies that have been circulating through the years. Just take a look at this fascinating translation of that passage:

> *Jesus said, "Do not think I came to annul, to bring an incorrect interpretation to the Torah or the Prophets: I did not come to annul but to bring spiritual abundance, for the Torah to be obeyed as it should be and God's promises to receive fulfillment. For truly I say to you: until the sky and the Earth would pass away, not one yod or one vav could ever pass away from the Torah, until everything would come to pass. Therefore, whoever would break one of the least of these commandments, and would teach people this way, will be called the least in the kingdom of heaven: but whoever would do the commandments and would teach them, will be called great in the kingdom of heaven."*
>
> ~ Matthew 5:17-19, PNT

Here there is a huge key in the words *"for the Torah to be obeyed as it should be and God's promises to receive fulfillment."* Even in that day, man had put his interpretation on the model God had given in His Word!

This Scripture is often used to tell the Church that they are no longer under the Law. A better way to express that Scripture is to understand that we are no longer subject to the *penalty* of the Law.

Yeshua/Jesus paid that penalty once and for all with His blood. He Himself says:

> *"The scribes and the Pharisees have seated themselves in the chair of Moses; therefore all that they tell you, do and observe, but do not do according to their deeds; for they say things and do not do them. They tie up heavy burdens and lay them on men's shoulders, but they themselves are unwilling to move them with so much as a finger."*

> ~ Matthew 23:2-4

Yeshua/Jesus cautions the people not to stray from the teachings of Moses given to the world by God, but to beware of the teachings of men. Back then, the Jewish leaders had imposed "fence laws" that kept the people *penned in* because of works not required by the Lord.

So now you may be asking, "What is a fence law?" Let me tell you.

The generations before the New Testament had a collection of sayings and writings that they felt were essential to understanding the Torah. Sadly, they considered these writings equal in power to the written Word of God and sometimes higher and more authoritative. It was believed God gave an oral law along with the written Law He gave Moses and that the written law could not be understood without the oral explanation. They spent much time writing how-tos for the people. These extra rules were called "fence laws" as they put a fence around the actual Word of God.

Let me give you an example. The Torah teaches: "Don't boil a kid in its mother's milk" (Exodus 23:19). The rabbis concluded that meant don't eat milk and meat. Well, here is the rub. When the Lord and two angels showed up to talk with Abraham one hot day in Mamre, Abraham served his guests the following menu: *"Curds and milk and the calf which he had prepared,"* along with freshly baked bread (Genesis 18:8). Sounds like milk and meat to me. Actually, that custom was a pagan custom, and I think the Lord was simply saying, "It's time to do things My way."

What is believed by many scholars today is that God was steering the Jewish community away from known pagan customs. According to various Bible commentaries, the pagans of that era practiced a fertility rite, which involved boiling a kid (a young calf) in its mother's milk and sprinkling the broth as a magic charm on their gardens and fields. They did this in the hope of increasing the yield of their crops.[1]

So, you can see why Jesus was upset with the rabbis. They were imposing heavy, unnecessary burdens while not teaching what God wanted the people to understand. Many denominations, both ancient and current, have followed this ill-advised method of controlling their parishioners. This is not the place or the time to name names, but I do encourage you to check out for yourself the teachings you are listening to and ask Holy Spirit for discernment.

Today the Church has committed similar sins—built walls instead of bridges to the love of God. These walls were created through bringing mixed interpretation/translation to the Word of God instead of the purity of His Word that He intended His adopted children to embrace. Often, that mixture comes to us in the form of tradition or false teachings, topics I will address in another chapter.

A Study in Messianic Prophecy

The following is a detailed document of the prophetic Scriptures of Jesus in the Old Testament, heralding the fulfillment of His coming in the New Testament. This chart was graciously given to us by Dr. Howard Morgan, the apostle who ordained me.

The chart starts with the following Scripture:

---

1 https://www.bibletools.org/index.cfm/fuseaction/Topical.show/RTD/cgg/ID/9313/
Boiling-Kid-its-Mothers-Milk.htm

Then said I, "Lo, I come: in the volume of the book it is written of me, I delight to do thy will, O my God; yea, thy law is within my heart."

~ Psalm 40:7-8, KJV

The full understanding of who Yeshua/Jesus is and what He came to accomplish can only be realized if we receive the "volume of the book." Of Yeshua/Jesus, John writes:

In the beginning was the Word, and the Word was with God, and the Word was God. He was in the beginning with God. All things came into being through Him, and apart from Him nothing came into being that has come into being. In Him was life, and the life was the Light of men. The Light shines in the darkness, and the darkness did not *comprehend it.

~ John 1:1-5

A BIBLICAL STUDY IN MESSIANIC PROPHECY

Then said I, "Lo, I come: in the volume of the book it is written of me, I delight to do thy will, O my God; yea, thy law is within my heart."

~Psalm 40:7, 8

FULFILLED PROPHECY	TANAKH/ HEBREW SCRIPTURE	NEW TESTAMENT
MESSIAH'S ANCESTRY		
His pre-existence	Micah 5:2	John 1:1,14
Born of the seed of a woman	Genesis 3:15	Matthew 1:18
Of the seed of Abraham	Genesis 12:3	Matthew 1:1-16
All nations blessed by Abraham's seed	Genesis 12:3, 22:18	Matthew 8:5,10; Galatians 3:16
God would provide Himself a Lamb as an offering.	Genesis 22:8	John 1:29
From the tribe of Judah	Genesis 49:10	Matthew 1:1-3; Hebrews 7:14; Revelation 5:5
Heir to the throne of David	2 Samuel 7:12-13; Jeremiah 33:17, 25:5-6; Isaiah 9:6-7	Matthew 1:1
THE DIVINE NATURE OF MESSIAH CONFIRMED		
For a child will be born to us, a son will be given to us; And the government will rest on His shoulders; And His name will be called Wonderful Counselor, Mighty God, Eternal Father, Prince of Peace.	Isaiah 9:6	Matthew 1:23

A BIBLICAL STUDY IN MESSIANIC PROPHECY

THE DIVINE NATURE OF MESSIAH CONFIRMED (CONTINUED)

The ruler of Israel born in Bethlehem. His going forth is from everlasting.	Micah 5:2	Matthew 2:1
His birth miraculous sign to be born of a virgin. He was to have a divine nature and called "Immanuel."	Isaiah 7:14	Matthew 1:18,23
Declared to be the Son of God. The King over the whole Earth is called "The Son of God." The Eternal God has a Son. Do you know His name?	Psalm 2:7 Proverbs 30:4	Matthew 3:17; 16:16, 17:5; Hebrews 1:5
Presented with gifts	Psalm 72:10	Matthew 2:1,11
Called out of Egypt	Hosea 11:1	Matthew 2:15
Slaughter of the children	Jeremiah 31:15	Matthew 2:18
Would be a Nazarene	Judges 13:5; Amos 2:11; Lamentations 4:7	Matthew 2:23

MESSIAH WAS TO HAVE A FORERUNNER

His messenger before Him in the spirit of Elijah	Malachi 4:5-6	Luke 1:17
Preceded by a messenger to prepare His way	Malachi 3:1	Matthew 11:7-11, 3:1-2; Luke 1:17
Messenger crying, "Prepare ye the way of the Lord."	Isaiah 40:3	Matthew 3:3

A BIBLICAL STUDY IN MESSIANIC PROPHECY

MESSIAH'S MINISTRY

Brought light to the lands of Zebulun and Naphtali, Galilee of the Gentiles	Isaiah 9:1-2	Matthew 4:15
Would be a prophet of the children of Israel	Deuteronomy 18:15	Matthew 2:15
Heal blind, deaf, lame, and dumb	Isaiah 35:5-6, 29:18	Matthew 11:5
Preached to the poor, brokenhearted, and captives	Isaiah 61:1	Matthew 11:5
Messiah bore our sickness	Isaiah 53:4	Matthew 8:16-17
Came to bring a sword, not peace	Micah 7:6	Matthew 10:34-35
Messiah was to teach in parables.	Psalm 78:2	Matthew 13:34-35
Messiah was to have a special anointing of the Holy Spirit.	Isaiah 11:2, 42:6-7, 61:1; Psalm 45:7	Matthew 3:16-17; Luke 4:16-21
Messiah was to be a prophet like unto Moses.	Deuteronomy 18:15-19	Acts 3:20-23; Luke 7:16; John 6:14-19
Messiah was to defeat satan.	Genesis 3:15	Galatians 4:4; 1 John 3:8
Messiah was to be a priest after the order of Melchizedek.	Psalm 110:4	Hebrews 5:5-6, 7:25; Romans 8:34
Messiah was to be a redeemer of the Gentiles as well as the Jews.	Isaiah 49:6,42:1,6	Matthew 12:18; Acts 10:45
Rejected by His own	Isaiah 53: 1-3,49:7; Psalm 69:9,118:22; Micah 5:1	Matthew 21:42; Mark 8:31, 12:10; Luke 9:22, 17:25; John 1:11,19:15; Luke 23:13-25
Jesus is the stone which the builders rejected which became the headstone.	Psalm 118:22-23; Isaiah 28:16	Matthew 21:42;1 Peter 2:7

A BIBLICAL STUDY IN MESSIANIC PROPHECY

MESSIAH'S MINISTRY (CONTINUED)

A stone of stumbling to Israel	Isaiah 8:14-15	1 Peter 2:8; Romans 9:31-33
Jesus entered Jerusalem as a King riding on an ass.	Zechariah 9:9	Matthew 21:1-11

EVENTS OF MESSIAH'S BETRAYAL, DEATH, RESURRECTION AND ASCENSION FORETOLD

Betrayed by a friend	Psalms 41:9	John 13: 13-21; Matthew 26:23-24
Sold for 30 pieces of silver	Zechariah 11:12	Matthew 26:15; Luke 22:5
The 30 pieces of silver given for the potter's field.	Zechariah 11:12	Matthew 27:9-10
The 30 pieces of silver thrown in the temple.	Zechariah 11:13	Matthew 27:5
Forsaken by His disciples	Zechariah 13:7	Matthew 26:56
Accused by false witnesses	Psalm 35:11	Matthew 26:60
Silent to accusations	Isaiah 53:7	Matthew 27:14
Spat upon, smitten, and scourged	Isaiah 50:6, 53:5	Matthew 27:26, 30,39-44; Mark 14:65, 15:19; Luke 22:63
Smitten on the cheek	Micah 5:1	Matthew 27:30
Hated without a cause	Psalm 35:19; 22:7-8	Matthew 27:23

A BIBLICAL STUDY IN MESSIANIC PROPHECY

EVENTS OF MESSIAH'S BETRAYAL, DEATH, RESURRECTION AND ASCENSION FORETOLD (CONTINUED)

The sacrificial lamb	Isaiah 53:5	John 1:29
Given for a covenant	Isaiah 42:6; Jeremiah 31:31-34	Romans 11:27; Galatians 3:17, 4:24; Hebrews 12:24; 13:20
Would not strive or cry	Isaiah 42:2-3	Mark 7:36
People would hear not and see not.	Isaiah 6:9-10	Matthew 13:14-15
People trust in traditions of men.	Isaiah 29:13	Matthew 15:9
People give God lip service.	Isaiah 29:13	Matthew 15:8
God delights in Him.	Isaiah 42:1	Matthew 3:17, 17:5
Wounded for our sins	Isaiah 53:5	John 6:51
He bore the sins of many.	Isaiah 53:10-12	Mark 10:45
Messiah not killed for Himself.	Daniel 9:26	Matthew 20:28
Gentiles flock to Him.	Isaiah 55:5, 60:3, 65:1; Malachi 1:11; 2 Samuel 22:44-45	Matthew 8:10
Crucified with criminals	Isaiah 53:9-12	Matthew 27:35-38
His body was pierced.	Zechariah 12:10; Psalm 22:16	John 20:25,27; Luke:23:33
Thirsty during execution	Psalm 22:115	John 19:28
Given vinegar and gall for thirst	Psalm 69:21	Matthew 27:34

A BIBLICAL STUDY IN MESSIANIC PROPHECY

EVENTS OF MESSIAH'S BETRAYAL, DEATH, RESURRECTION AND ASCENSION FORETOLD (CONTINUED)

Soldiers gambled for his garment.	Psalm 22:18	Matthew 27:35
People mocked, "He trusted in God, let Him deliver Him!"	Psalm 22:7-8	Matthew 27:43
People sat there looking at Him.	Psalm 22:17	Matthew 27:36
Cried, "My God, my God, why hast thou forsaken me?"	Psalm 22:1	Matthew 27:46
Darkness over the land	Amos 8:9	Matthew 27:45
No bones broken	Psalm 34:20; Numbers 9:12	John 19:33-36
Side pierced	Zechariah 12:10	John 19:34
Buried with the rich	Isaiah 53:9	Matthew 27:57,60
Resurrected from the dead	Psalm 16:10-11, 49:15; Isaiah 53:10	Mark 16:6; Acts 3:31,13:33-37
Priest after the order of Melchizedek	Psalm 110:4	Hebrews 5:5-6, 6:20; 7:15-17
Ascended to right hand of God	Psalm 68:18,	Luke 24:51
LORD said unto Him, "Sit thou at my right hand, until I make thine enemies thy footstool."	Psalm 110:1	Matthew 22:44; Mark 12:36, 16:19; Luke 20:42-43; Acts 2:34-35; Hebrews 1:13
His coming glory	Malachi 3:2-3	Luke 3:17

Study in Messianic Prophecy chart reprinted by permission: www.kingmin.org.

For, brothers, I want you to understand this truth which God formerly concealed but has now revealed, so that you won't imagine you know more than you actually do. It is that stoniness, to a degree, has come upon Isra'el , until the Gentile world enters in its fullness.

~ Romans 11:25, CJB

LEVEL PLAYING FIELD

Role of the Jewish and Gentile People

W HEN I STARTED LEARNING and teaching about Jewish roots, I renamed the class "Biblical Hebraic Teaching." But I kept running into walls of disagreement between Gentile believers and Jewish believers—walls of misunderstanding about Jewish roots. What I observed was the arrogance of both camps trying to push their understanding of how to interpret things they claimed as God's way. In this environment, there simply was no way for the One New Man to emerge. I can sincerely understand why those who were teaching about the One New Man so often said, "We don't know what it will look like."

The misunderstanding is nothing new, as I pointed out in Chapter 2 that the enmity or jealousy caused by the Torah was operating from early on between the Gentile and Jewish believers. Jesus addressed this issue in Matthew 5:17, stating clearly that He came to make sense of the Torah and how to abide by it, not abolish it. Paul addresses this same issue specifically in Romans 9-11.

We saw throughout the Old Testament that the role of the Jewish people is to be the preservers and models of the ways of God. In Romans, we see that the role of the Gentiles is also a fundamental key to God's plan. In fact, without them, there is no purpose for it. The ultimate goal was for the world to know God sent Jesus for the redemption of all mankind. The oneness that Jesus talks to the Father about in John 17 is the coming together of the Jewish people and the nations (the Gentiles) by understanding the heart of the Father through the demonstration of His Son.

In a conversation with my friend, Reverend Laura Moreland, she explained another cause of conflict:

"Many scholars believe that the church/congregation at Rome was founded by Jews returning to Rome from Pentecost (see Acts 2:1-12). Gentile believers joined the founding Jewish believers along with Jewish believers in that region. In the early church, most of the leadership were Jewish believers who knew how to worship the God of Abraham, Isaac, and Jacob and had firsthand knowledge of what was taught by Peter, Paul, and the other apostles about Messiah Yeshua. By late 40 a.d., there was a lot of persecution experienced by the Christians and Jews in Rome. However, the Church flourished, even though their monotheistic belief (One God) was in conflict with the expected worship of the Roman emperor Claudius. This resulted in Emperor Claudius banishing all the Jews from Rome in 49 a.d. This decree lasted five years and, during this time, leadership roles were filled in the Roman church by the Gentile believers. After five years of exile, the Jewish believers came back to the church in Rome to take their former place of leadership. The now established Gentile believers did not want to give up the leadership so there was a conflict in the church between the Jewish believers and the Gentile believers, which Paul is addressing in the letter of Romans."

To give credit where credit is due, the greatest orchestrator of this division is Satan. He knows that unity will validate that Jesus was sent by God and that truth will destroy Satan's plans. We also know that pride in believers is the legal access of Satan into their understanding.

The book of Romans clarifies that salvation is received by faith and able to sanctify both Jews and Gentiles. Unfortunately, pride is still causing separation in the Church. It has several doctrinal names that will be covered in the following chapter.

You saw the intent of the Father's heart for unity, clearly laid out in Ephesians 2. In Romans 11, we learn from Paul's writings how God chose to deal with the jealousy by creating a level playing field and making it clear that each people group could not be in God's will without the other. To get a clear picture, it is best to start at Romans 9.

Value of the Jewish People

Not unlike Moses, Paul starts out in Romans 9, declaring his heart for the people of God that are his natural bloodline:

> *I am telling the truth in Christ, I am not lying, my conscience testifies with me in the Holy Spirit, that I have great sorrow and unceasing grief in my heart. For I could wish that I myself were accursed, separated from Christ for the sake of my brethren, my kinsmen according to the flesh, who are Israelites, to whom belongs the adoption as sons, and the glory and the covenants and the giving of the Law and the temple service and the promises, whose are the fathers, and from whom is the Christ according to the flesh, who is over all, God blessed forever. Amen.*

> Romans 9:1-5

Now clearly, Paul is making the case that the Jewish people hold a valued position in God's Kingdom—so much so that he is willing to give up his salvation for theirs. Do you remember Moses, too, pleaded for Israel, at the risk of his life? He carried, without reservation, the heart of the Father. It causes me to pause and examine my own heart.

Please remember: The value of the Jewish people is that God loves them and chose them to reveal His plan to the world. However, all that is theirs can be yours; without them, there would be nothing for you, including Jesus. Think on that for a while.

Paul has already stated:

For I am not ashamed of the gospel, for it is the power of God for salvation to everyone who believes, to the Jew first and also to the Greek. For in it the righteousness of God is revealed from faith to faith; as it is written, "BUT THE RIGHTEOUS MAN SHALL LIVE BY FAITH."

~ Romans 1:16-17

So, we are clear that the righteousness of God is by faith. Abraham was considered righteous because of faith. Yet, why does Paul mention that it is to the Jew first? If the Gospel is another name for good news, from Genesis to Revelation, that good news was given first to the Jew so they could share it with the world. Their story, including the New Testament, was written under the inspiration of the Holy Spirit *about* the Jewish people and their Jewish Messiah by Jewish people.

That being said, the big question is: Why have the majority of Jewish people rejected Jesus as the Messiah, even in the time of Paul? This is what Paul is beginning to address in Romans 9:6-8, NASB 1995:

But it is not as though the word of God has failed. For they are not all Israel who are descended from Israel; nor are they all children because they are Abraham's descendants, but: "THROUGH ISAAC YOUR DESCENDANTS WILL BE NAMED." That is, it is not the children of the flesh who are children of God, but the children of the promise are regarded as descendants.

May I pose a question here? First, we know that the children of the first promise are Isaac and his descendants. Natural Israel has that calling. Romans 11:29 tells us nothing can change that because the Jewish people's calling is irrevocable. However, the Gentiles who believe in Yeshua/Jesus also receive the stated promise of blessing in Genesis 12 when God tells Abram *"through you all the nations of the world will be blessed."* (vs. 3). As we read here in Romans 9, we see God will include the Gentile nations in the promised blessing of sonship through the shed blood of Yeshua/Jesus.

What if God, although willing to demonstrate His wrath and to make His power known, endured with much patience vessels of wrath prepared for destruction? And He did so to make known the riches of His glory upon vessels of mercy, which He prepared beforehand for glory, even us, whom He also called, not from among Jews only, but also from among Gentiles.

As He says also in Hosea,

"I WILL CALL THOSE WHO WERE NOT MY PEOPLE, 'MY PEOPLE,' AND HER WHO WAS NOT BELOVED, 'BELOVED.' "AND IT SHALL BE THAT IN THE PLACE WHERE IT WAS SAID TO THEM, 'YOU ARE NOT MY PEOPLE,' THERE THEY SHALL BE CALLED SONS OF THE LIVING GOD."

~ Romans 9:22-26

To this, I declare with Paul: *"Oh, the depth of the riches both of the wisdom and knowledge of God! How unsearchable are His judgments and unfathomable His ways! FOR WHO HAS KNOWN THE MIND OF THE LORD, OR WHO BECAME HIS COUNSELOR?" (Romans 11:33-34).*

Truly, as we continue in these chapters, you will again hear these words of Romans 11:33 resounding in your spirit. God operates so far outside the box of our understanding. Thank You, Lord, that this is so!

Grace vs. Works—Truth for All

Our loving God has made a level playing field in the understanding of who He is so no one people group can boast of being superior. Rather, each one has a divine purpose as God calls them to come and sit at His table and be adopted into His family.

> *What shall we say then? That Gentiles, who did not pursue righteousness, attained righteousness, even the righteousness which is by faith; but Israel, pursuing a law of righteousness, did not arrive at that law. Why? Because they did not pursue it by faith, but as though it were by works.*

They stumbled over the stumbling stone, just as it is written,

> *"BEHOLD, I LAY IN ZION A STONE OF STUMBLING AND A ROCK OF OFFENSE, AND HE WHO BELIEVES IN HIM WILL NOT BE DISAPPOINTED."*

~ Romans 9:30-33

I believe Paul was making a clear point that salvation is by grace, not works. Was he then specifically addressing the Jewish people alive in Yeshua's/Jesus' time? There was an issue with some Jewish believers that, although they believed that salvation was by faith, they held tightly to the law for sanctification, whereas Gentile believers, not familiar with the Torah, felt that Jesus was enough and that they had no restrictions.

Sadly, we see that in the Body of Christ today. Some of those who have embraced their Jewish roots are walking out their faith through laws and traditions they impose on themselves instead of letting the Holy Spirit lead them by the model of His Word through God's calendar and appointed times. Others in the Church are embracing what has now been termed *hyper-grace,* setting no moral godly standards and giving way to worldly wisdom outside of God's Word.

I do believe there were Jewish people throughout the Bible who truly loved the Lord and offered sacrifices by faith that produce redemption. Abraham is the clearest example, for he was considered righteous because of his faith. Many of the biblical stories in the Word show us individuals who had a faith-based relationship with God. Perhaps those are the ones Yeshua/Jesus redeemed when He went to Hell and preached the Gospel after His death on the cross.

I believe, according to the Word, that there has always been a righteous remnant that had a righteous bloodline. It is possible that those who accepted Jesus when He was on the Earth came from a line of true lovers of God. We have heard much teaching about iniquitous bloodline issues that we can take to the courts of Heaven and receive healing for our family. How much more can we call forth our blessings from the righteous bloodlines?

Please, Help My Brothers!

Paul again makes a plea for the salvation of his kinsmen, appealing to Gentile believers to reach out to his people:

> *Brethren, my heart's desire and my prayer to God for them is for their salvation. For I testify about them that they have a zeal for God, but not in accordance with knowledge. For not knowing about God's righteousness and seeking to establish their own, they did not subject themselves to the righteousness of God. For Christ is the end of the law for righteousness to everyone who believes.*
>
> ~ Romans 10:1-4

"Not in accordance with knowledge" is a very telling statement. The unbelieving Jews did not realize that the penalty for sin paid by Jesus on the cross was the only way to righteousness. It was through His shed blood that God gave the world opportunity to enter into the everlasting covenant when God would write His laws on their hearts and they would know Him (see Jeremiah 31).

> *For with the heart a person believes, resulting in righteousness, and with the mouth he confesses, resulting in salvation. For the Scripture says, "WHOEVER BELIEVES IN HIM WILL NOT BE DISAPPOINTED" For there is no distinction between Jew and Greek; for the same Lord is Lord of all, abounding in riches for all who call on Him; for "WHOEVER WILL CALL ON THE NAME OF THE LORD WILL BE SAVED."*
>
> ~ Romans 10:10-13

Yet, once more, Paul calls on the believers to speak truth to the Jewish people:

> *How then will they call on Him in whom they have not believed? How will they believe in Him whom they have not heard? And how will they hear without a preacher?*
>
> ~ Romans 10:14

Remember, as previously stated, the first believers were predominantly Jewish, for Christ said, "I have come for the lost sheep of Israel," sending the initial disciples out only to the Jewish community. As I explained in the previous chapter, the Jews were created to be a light to the world and reveal the salvation plan. However, as The Plan unfolds in greater detail, God gives the Gentiles the same opportunity to reach back and share the Gospel with the Jewish nation.

The following Scriptures are part of the great mystery, for although God continued to call to the Jewish people, He "blinded" them in part (as we will see in Romans 11) so that the Gentiles could partake of the blessings.

> *However, they did not all heed the good news; for Isaiah says, "LORD, WHO SHALL RECEIVE OUR REPORT" So faith comes from hearing, and hearing by the word of Christ. But I say, surely, they have never heard, have they? Indeed, they have; "THEIR VOICE HAS GONE OUT INTO ALL THE EARTH, AND THEIR WORDS TO THE END OF THE WORLD." But I say, surely Israel did not know, did they? First Moses says, "I WILL MAKE YOU JEALOUS BY THAT WHICH IS NOT A NATION, BY A NATION WITHOUT UNDERSTANDING WILL I ANGER YOU" And Isaiah is very bold and says, "I WAS FOUND BY THOSE WHO DID NOT SEEK ME, I BECAME MANIFEST TO THOSE WHO DID NOT ASK FOR ME." But as for Israel He says, "ALL THE DAY LONG I HAVE STRETCHED OUT MY HANDS TO A DISOBEDIENT AND OBSTINATE PEOPLE"*
>
> ~ Romans 10:16-21

So, who is God speaking about through Moses that He will use to make the Jewish people jealous? And where does that leave the Jews? Read on.

Not Forgotten, Still Beloved

> *I say then, God has not rejected His people, has He? May it never be! For I too am an Israelite, a descendant of Abraham, of the tribe of Benjamin. God has not rejected His people whom He foreknew.*
>
> ~ Romans 11:1-2

I, too, am a descendant of Abraham of the tribe of Judah with a call to the Ekklesia like Paul. The number of Jewish believers grows daily, current evidence that God is truly not finished with us yet.

> *I say then, they did not stumble so as to fall, did they? May it never be! But by their transgression salvation has come to the Gentiles, to make them jealous.*

> ~ Romans 11:11

We need to let this sink in. Salvation has come to the Gentiles to make the Jews jealous. One interesting point—this statement fulfills the prophecy of Deuteronomy 32:31 as quoted in Romans 10:19.

Let us clarify the meaning of *transgression*. The Greek translation of *transgression* is the word *paraptom*, meaning "fault, a mistake or an error." Israel's mistake was they rejected righteousness by faith, not believing Jesus was the Messiah. However, not all rejected Him; God had his remnant. Paul tells us they stumbled but did not fall. Interestingly, one commentator remarks that Paul is saying they did not fall out of sight of the Lord. They remain the apple of His eye. In other words, contrary to some believers' opinions, God is not done with Israel.

It may seem odd that God would choose to use this method to open salvation to the Gentile. Yet, the strategy of the Almighty transcends our simple understanding of justice. Here is where the level playing field comes into play.

> *Now if their transgression is riches for the world and their failure is riches for the Gentiles, how much more will their fulfillment be! But I am speaking to you who are Gentiles. Inasmuch then as I am an apostle of Gentiles, I magnify my ministry, if somehow, I might move to jealousy my fellow countrymen and save some of them.*

> ~ Romans 11:12-14

Okay, we now know that the transgression of the Jewish people was a misstep that caused them to stumble, but not to utterly fall. Their misstep was purposed by God to bring opportunity to the world to be partakers of salvation. Let's keep in mind that He gave the opportunity first to the Jews to receive the truth of God's Word and ways and to be the natural bloodline of Yeshua/Jesus. He also gave them the first opportunity to share the good news with the Gentiles. Now, through their "stumbling," He is giving that rich opportunity to the Gentiles to follow in the footsteps of the Jews and bring the Gospel back to the rest of the world.

Unfortunately, the Gentiles had their own misstep as is evident today. They put more energy into sharing the good news with the other nations than with the Jewish people. They missed the end of the verse above that says, *"How much more will their fulfillment be!"*

May I say here their fulfillment is not only recognition of their Messiah but also the understanding of God's heart for the nations (the Gentiles) and their call to be that light.

Paul is clearly stating when the Jewish people regain their footing and understand the truth of God's full plan, there is going to be a fullness not yet obtained. Let's not leave Satan out of this picture. He has been working feverishly to prevent The Plan by instigating hatred of the Jewish people to bring about the extinction of their race. Throughout church history, he has created doctrines of demons to sabotage God's plan and continues the hatred as a means of separation to prevent the One New Man.

For if their rejection is the reconciliation of the world, what will their acceptance be but life from the dead?

~ Romans 11:15

I have pondered what Paul means when he says, "life from the dead." Could it be life from dead works? An understanding that the doing of the law to bring about redemption is now replaced with the law written on the heart? The fulfillment of Jeremiah 31.

> *"Behold, days are coming," declares the LORD, "when I will make a new covenant with the house of Israel and with the house of Judah, not like the covenant which I made with their fathers in the day I took them by the hand to bring them out of the land of Egypt, My covenant which they broke, although I was a husband to them," declares the LORD. "But this is the covenant which I will make with the house of Israel after those days," declares the LORD, "I will put My law within them and on their heart I will write it; and I will be their God, and they shall be My people. "They will not teach again, each man his neighbor and each man his brother, saying, 'Know the LORD,' for they will all know Me, from the least of them to the greatest of them," declares the LORD, "for I will forgive their iniquity, and their sin I will remember no more."*
>
> ~ Jeremiah 31:31-34,

Can you imagine what joy that will bring the Father to have His firstborn sons of Israel back home in the Father's house alongside the nations? Remember that He created the Jewish people to reveal His plan to the world. He is waiting to be gracious to us all. What is He waiting for? Their repentance.

> *Therefore the LORD longs to be gracious to you, and therefore He waits on high to have compassion on you. For the LORD is a God of justice; How blessed are all those who long for Him. O people in Zion, inhabitant in Jerusalem, you will weep no longer. He will surely be gracious to you at the sound of your cry; when He hears it, He will answer you.*
>
> ~ Isaiah 30:18-19

Gentiles—Grafted into the Vine

Let's continue looking at Romans as we explore the explanation of "grafted in"—a term you hear continually when there is teaching about the One New Man. The following is key to understanding God's plan. Paul is using the example of the olive tree to bring revelation to his hearers of God's plan for the Commonwealth of Israel as revealed in Ephesians 2.

References to the olive tree are found throughout the Bible. I was amazed as I researched the web how many sites ignore the representation of the olive tree as the Commonwealth of Israel. These sites use this teaching as a picture of our intimacy with the Lord. This is typical of those who do not understand that God did not replace Israel with the Church.

First, we have to come to an understanding of the root of the olive tree. God calls it "holy."

> *If the first piece of dough is holy, the lump is also; and if the root is holy, the branches are too.*
>
> ~ Romans 11:16

The Hebrew word for *holy* is *qodesh*, which means set apart from the ordinary. For example, the first thing God called "holy" in the Bible is the Sabbath. Not man or creation; He called those things "good." But a period of time called Sabbath, He declares is set apart from the ordinary. It is not the opposite of evil, for the six other days in the week are not evil, but ordinary. God is set apart from man. He transcends every possible ordinary part of life on the planet.

The Greek word for *holy* is *hagios*, which also means "set apart, sacred, and worthy of respect."

Thus, the olive tree picture is far from ordinary. So, what is the root? Some say it is Yeshua/Jesus. Some say it is the Word of God. Still, others say it is the Jewish people who are the carriers of the

Word of God, which is Jesus incarnate. Therefore, I say it is all of the above; you cannot separate them. In light of the Greek definition "worthy of respect," Genesis 12 becomes ever clearer when God says you will be cursed if you take the Jewish people for granted.

Read the following with this in mind: The broken-off branches are the Jewish people who have not yet accepted Jesus as Messiah, and the wild olive branches are the Gentile people who have.

> *But if some of the branches were broken off, and you, being a wild olive, were grafted in among them and became partaker with them of the rich root of the olive tree, do not be arrogant toward the branches; but if you are arrogant, remember that it is not you who supports the root, but the root supports you. You will say then, "Branches were broken off so that I might be grafted in." Quite right, they were broken off for their unbelief, but you stand by your faith. Do not be conceited, but fear; for if God did not spare the natural branches, He will not spare you, either.*
>
> ~ Romans 11:17-21

Paul is being very clear: God is a God of justice. He has devised a plan of equal opportunity for all mankind. As we read on, we will see how merciful He is.

> *Behold then the kindness and severity of God; to those who fell, severity, but to you, God's kindness, if you continue in His kindness; otherwise you also will be cut off. And they also, if they do not continue in their unbelief, will be grafted in, for God is able to graft them in again. For if you were cut off from what is by nature a wild olive tree, and were grafted contrary to nature into a cultivated olive tree, how much more will these who are the natural branches be grafted into their own olive tree?*
>
> ~ Romans 11:22-24

What is the kindness He is encouraging the Gentile believers to continue in? It is the greatest thing you can offer anyone. It is the sharing of the Gospel. This passage also points out how God is a God of redemption, offering a place of repentance, which simply means to turn back or turn around to the truth of His love.

Tod McDowell uses the term cycle of revival—the Jewish people revealing God's truth to the nations and the call of the nations to reveal The Plan back to the Jewish nation. Unfortunately, as the Church has gone out to bring the Gospel to worldwide people groups, they have, for the most part, failed to make it a priority to spread the truth to the Jewish people due to wrong understanding.

Let's go back for a minute to Romans 11:15: *"For if their rejection is the reconciliation of the world, what will their acceptance be but life from the dead?"*

Could life from the dead also mean a fresh outpouring of the Holy Spirit on the Ekklesia (Church) when the Jewish people understand the fullness of God's plan? What would that look like? Greater signs and wonders as in the early church when the Jewish people were in leadership? What would it look like when the Jewish people stepped back into the role they were created for—the role to be the light to the nations? After all, that is their very DNA, their "Divine Nature Aptitude." Could their acceptance be the key to the Third Great Awakening (the final harvest)?

Can you see why Satan has been working overtime to destroy the Jewish people? Not just their lives, but also their spiritual anointing.

Paul continues to bring absolute clarity to the Gentiles of their position and role in the end-game plan and how merciful God is.

For I do not want you, brethren, to be uninformed of this mystery—so that you will not be wise in your own estimation—that a partial hardening has happened to Israel until the fullness of the Gentiles has come in.

~ Romans 11:25

Who could understand the ways of God to bring a partial hardening until the "fullness of the Gentiles?" This fullness has been so misrepresented. I do not believe it is the full number of those who will name the name of Jesus.

I believe it is the fullness of the understanding of God's heart for The Plan that puts the Jewish people and Israel center stage. Center stage as the preserver of the Word of God so that the nations could receive His Son. Center stage as the natural bloodline of Yeshua/Jesus to show the world God's mercy and His ways. Center stage in the role of the Gentiles to reach back with the Gospel to the Jewish people. Center stage that the land of Israel is where the Lord God has placed His name and continues to use it as a testing ground as to whether we will love what He loves. The way He loves without compromise for their sin, but with abounding love nevertheless.

The Scripture continues:

...and so all Israel will be saved; just as it is written.

~ Romans 11:26

Many authors have written various interpretations of the words "all Israel will be saved." May I suggest based on the fact this verse is in the context of this chapter, which represents the heart of the Father for the unity of the Jewish people and the Gentiles, that "all Israel" is the Commonwealth of Israel. Gentiles will not be replacing Israel but walking alongside her with the commonality of the covenant and the blood of Jesus making us One New Humanity—a dwelling place for God, according to Ephesians 2.

AND HE CAME AND PREACHED PEACE TO YOU WHO WERE FAR AWAY, AND PEACE TO YOU WHO WERE NEAR; for through Him we both have our access in one Spirit to the Father. So then you are no longer strangers and aliens, but you are fellow citizens with the saints, and are of God's household, having been built on the foundation of the apostles and prophets, Christ Jesus Himself being the cornerstone, in whom the whole building, being fitted together, is growing into a holy temple in the Lord, in whom you also are being built together into a dwelling of God in the Spirit.

~ Ephesians 2:17-22

Continuing in Romans 11, we see Jeremiah 31 restated:

"THE DELIVERER WILL COME FROM ZION, HE WILL REMOVE UNGODLINESS FROM JACOB." "THIS IS MY COVENANT WITH THEM, WHEN I TAKE AWAY THEIR SINS."

~ Romans 11:26-27

Here now is the final revelation of the role of each part of this new humanity, created out of the existing humanity of this planet to become the One New Man.

Here is the summary of the level playing field God has created in His love.

From the standpoint of the gospel they [the Jewish people] are enemies for your sake, but from the standpoint of God's choice they are beloved for the sake of the fathers; for the gifts and the calling of God are irrevocable. For just as you [Gentile] once were disobedient to God, but now have been shown mercy because of their disobedience, so these also now have been disobedient, that because of the mercy shown to you they also may now be shown mercy. For God has shut up all in disobedience so that He may show mercy to all.

Oh, the depth of the riches both of the wisdom and knowledge of God! How unsearchable are His judgments and unfathomable His ways! FOR WHO HAS KNOWN THE MIND OF THE LORD, OR WHO BECAME HIS COUNSELOR? OR WHO HAS FIRST GIVEN TO HIM THAT IT MIGHT BE PAID BACK TO HIM AGAIN? For from Him and through Him and to Him are all things. To Him be the glory forever. Amen.

~Romans 11:28-36, [author insert]

Amen and amen! Mercy to all....

Casting down arguments and every
high thing that exalts itself against the
knowledge of God,
bringing every thought into captivity
to the obedience of Christ.
~ 2 Corinthians 10:5

THE GREAT DECEPTION

THERE HAVE BEEN MANY names given to Satan's methods throughout the history of planet Earth. Some of his ways are subtle, some are cruel, but one is specifically purposed to destroy the value or the existence of Israel and God's firstborn sons, the Jewish race.

In this chapter, I hope to bring an understanding of that method. My prayer is that this understanding will safeguard you and those in your sphere of influence from falling prey to the deception that has been Satan's plan since the early Church fathers. False doctrine is created through misrepresenting God's instructions in His Word. A little twist here and there, a partial truth or a misplacement of truth is the method to bring the wrong interpretation of the truth.

At the core of Satan's method is a goal to get us to question God's Word and His ways. In the Garden with Eve, he poses a question about God's instruction to her and pulls on her weakness of pride, which I believe is at the root of all our sin. Certainly, it is what causes us not to trust Him, thinking we might just have a better way of doing things. And this is just what captured Eve's thoughts:

> *Now the serpent was craftier than any beast of the field which the Lord God had made. And he said to the woman, "Indeed, has God said, 'You shall not eat from any tree of the garden'?" The woman said to the serpent, "From the fruit of the trees of the garden we may eat; but from the fruit of the tree which is in the middle of the garden, God has said, 'You shall not eat from it or touch it, or you will die.'" The serpent said to the woman, "You surely will not die! For God knows that in the day you eat from it your eyes will be opened, and you will be like God, knowing good and evil."*

> ~ Genesis 3:1-5

In the last verse, Satan put his spin on God's intent. Satan wanted to *be* God, and that desire destroyed what he once possessed as one of Heaven's chief angels. Now, in revenge, he wants to destroy everything important to God. Keep that in mind as we look at all the ways Satan has attacked the Jewish people, Israel, and the Church. Remember, he was probably privy to the plans of God because he was the one who brought worship before God's throne.

> *"You were the anointed cherub who covers, and I placed you there. You were on the holy mountain of God; You walked in the midst of the stones of fire. You were blameless in your ways from the day you were created until unrighteousness was found in you."*

> ~ Ezekiel 28:14-15

Satan was in the perfect environment in Heaven. He was blameless. Then he fell. All creatures God created for fellowship with Him were given free will to choose that fellowship. But there will always be an opportunity to miss the mark with God. We see it in the Garden with Adam and Eve. We see it after the Flood. We see it throughout the Word of God as the story of the Jewish people is recorded in the Old and New Testaments. Today, in our current society, the evidence of conflict between God's ways and Satan's is becoming even more painfully clear as we see the wheat and tares (see Matthew 13) growing up together. Our protection against missteps is the written Word of God, the gift of power through the Holy Spirit to obey that Word, coupled with our willingness to submit.

Satan had fellowship with Jesus whom we know as the Living Word of God. He had access to the person of the Holy Spirit as well. Yet he chose not to submit to their counsel. We have that same choice daily.

Reading Ezekiel 28, it occurred to me that all the satanic and new age worship of walking over coals of fire was a representative action of what Satan did before the throne of God in His glory.

You were the anointed cherub who covers, and I placed you there. You were on the holy mountain of God.

~ Ezekiel 28:14

What an eye-opener! Satan was driven by his need to recapture what he lost by perverting, in every way possible, God's creations and God's plans.

May I tell you about a beautiful revelation about the fiery stones shared by a very good friend who has been called by God to be a prophetic worship warrior, Reverend Laurie Wong.

In a time of worship, Laurie heard the Lord invite her to come up higher and walk among the fiery stones. With that divine directive, she did some research. She learned from commentators that the "fiery stones" represent the living stones of mankind as a unique expression of the nations.

This revelation of the nations is based on the twelve stones in the ephod of the high priest's garment, which represents the twelve tribes of Israel. This garment was worn as the priest interceded before the mercy seat in the Holy of Holies. Let's keep in mind the fact that God offers all nations the opportunity to become part of the Commonwealth of Israel through the blood of Yeshua, as expressed in Ephesians 2

Laurie's understanding was that Satan's position in worship was to bring the intercession of the fulfillment of God's will for each nation. As a prophetic worshiper, my friend accepted God's invitation to intercede from that strategic place in the heavenlies to bring forth the destiny of the Kingdom of God on Earth as it is in Heaven.

Satan's Toolkit

Deception is the chief tool that Satan has devised to prevent God's will on Earth concerning Israel and the Jewish people. For example, the practice of injecting false doctrine throughout the teachings of the Church was originally named "Replacement Theology" or "Supersessionism." More recently, we hear the term "Fulfillment Theology." This term, while less condemnatory in tone, is nonetheless intended to displace the Jewish people from their God-intended destiny.

I believe the only way to be able to identify Replacement Theology as we encounter it, is to have a strong foundation of the truth of God's Word concerning the Jewish people and His plans for Israel and the Church.

When you truly grasp why God called Israel the "apple [pupil] of His eye" (see Psalm 17:8, author insert), you will understand that

God gave us the story of Israel recorded in the Bible from Genesis to Revelation to be a lens through which we view His heart, His ways, and His Son. When that lens is in place, you will find how often false doctrine is woven among truth from pulpits across America and around the globe. As a result, the hearer may unknowingly embrace the tenets of the incorrect or incomplete teaching that is a form of Replacement Theology.

In defense of many pastors, I want to be clear: their love for the Lord may be genuine while it is the interpretation of His ways that may have been handed down incorrectly, perhaps for generations.

As we become more aware of this error, we must also guard our hearts against arrogance and our tongues from overzealousness. We must hear clearly from the Lord how to pray for those in error. In presenting the truth in humility, we must not use our knowledge to judge or condemn, nor can we compromise the truth as we have come to understand it. It is imperative to be led by the Spirit as to how and when to share. Take it from one who has made a lot of huge mistakes and often picked up or caused a spirit of offense—another weapon the enemy can use to shut us down.

Anti-Semitism on the Rise

Merriam-Webster.com Dictionary tells us: Anti-Semitism is "hostility toward or discrimination against Jews as a religious, ethnic, or racial group."[1]

As a Jewish believer in Yeshua/Jesus, I have a more personal definition. If the Jewish people are the apple of God's eye and precious to Him; if His picture book through our Bible reveals the plan of His heart to send His Son Jesus Christ so that all the world might be saved, including *me*—Joanie—then it is appropriate to say anti-Semitism is anti-Christ.

---

[1] Merriam-Webster.com Dictionary, s.v. "anti-Semitism," accessed February 27, 2021, https://www.merriam-webster.com/dictionary/anti-Semitism.

Today, in the news, you can read or hear about shootings in temples and defacing of graves—violent acts—we would not expect here in the USA. However, my dear reader, the core prejudice against Jewish people is very real in my life and the lives of my Jewish friends. Most of us, throughout grade school, had to defend ourselves against the lie of being Christ-killers. I am in my seventies, so you do the math. I was told by someone twenty years younger that a swastika was painted on their locker in a suburban community high school.

When I attended an AIPAC (American Israel Public Affairs Council) conference in Washington D.C. in 2018, Jewish college students were asking for help as they felt threatened on their campuses. Those up-front expressions of hate are nothing new. I remember 15 years ago a student body organization at a state college sent out a flyer stating, "You can't kill Jews here in America, but you can support those around the globe who can!" Therefore, the USA is not the only place anti-Semitism is rising; this is a global issue. It has been recorded that anti-Semitism is at the same level of hatred worldwide as during Adolph Hitler's era.

There are ever more subtle expressions, too. Recently, in a conversation with a new and dear friend, she used the term, "Jew her down." This common phrase is used to characterize Jewish people as individuals who use unfair business practices. It never even crossed her mind that it was an offensive expression. When I explained that she was characterizing all Jewish people with a hurtful statement passed down from generations, she was caught off guard and very sorry. Yet, this unfortunate term clearly defames a people group.

Let me add here another piece of revelation God showed me on how the enemy has used human weakness to further his cause. We know unforgiveness in every situation causes bondage to all parties concerned. Here is a clear picture of how Satan has used it concerning the Jewish people. This is only one part of Satan's global strategy to destroy the people group that God chose to bring salvation to the world.

Approximately 12 years ago Chuck Pierce[2] asked me to light the Shabbat candles at a gathering in New Jersey. In preparation for that request, I received a word from the Lord to sing the prayer in a nontraditional way. The Lord gave me the melody by the Spirit. Sometime after that gathering, I went on an intercessory tour to Poland with Dr. Howard Morgan. The melody God gave me to sing as I light the Shabbat candles became known to those I was traveling with as "the lullaby" for the lost Jewish souls. I was asked to sing it over several places. I sang it over the graves throughout our tour and over the ashes in Birkenau, one of the infamous concentration camps where the ovens were continually burning, and the ashes were dumped in a pit. One day I was asked to sing at a manhole cover in Warsaw. That manhole was where they snuck the children of the ghetto out to get food. It was extremely dangerous for them. As I stood there and sang the melody, I heard the cries of the children's fear. I saw the anger of the parents shaking their fists to God and hatred to the Germans who were subjecting their families to such horror. I saw that the bitterness, anger, and unforgiveness was being trapped in a net in the Second Heaven and was fueling the demons to engage in promoting anti-Semitism. As I stood there, I was prompted by Holy Spirit to forgive the German people and address with forgiveness the anger my people had toward them and God. As I did this, I saw holes were made in the net that was holding the hatred that fueled the demonic realm. I was reminded of Corrie ten Boom's story of forgiveness.

Satan's Target: Women—Carriers of the Seed

Satan started with Eve in the Garden of Eden, stealing her position of authority with a lie. He knew the Redeemer would come through a woman and the people group called the Hebrews, so his first objective was to destroy the seed. Could it also be that the

---

[2] Chuck Pierce is president of Glory of Zion Ministries International, a ministry that aligns Jew and Gentile.

enmity between Cain and Abel was orchestrated to kill the seed of the woman? Consider the oppression of women through the ages. Perhaps Satan has always targeted women as carriers of the seed, a God-honored position.

Throughout the history of the Jewish people, there have been attempts to wipe out the Jewish race. Wars of kings against Jerusalem. Pointed destruction of the race found in the stories of Esther and Hanukkah. The root cause of these attacks against the Jewish nation was always the worship of their God.

Some wars were brought about because of Israel's sin and the need for God's discipline to bring them back to Him. God longed to be gracious to this people group, but insisted that they repent of their rebellion:

> *Therefore the LORD longs to be gracious to you, and therefore He waits on high to have compassion on you. For the LORD is a God of justice; how blessed are all those who long for Him.*
>
> ~ Isaiah 30:18

His mercy was clear, for although he often used the nations to discipline His people, He was not happy when these Nations went too far.

> *So the angel who was speaking with me said to me, "Proclaim, saying, 'Thus says the LORD of hosts, "I am exceedingly jealous for Jerusalem and Zion. But I am very angry with the nations who are at ease; for while I was only a little angry, they furthered the disaster."*
>
> ~ Zechariah 1:14-15

Along with wars, history records that Satan has continually targeted the next generation. Early in Israel's history, he tempted them with infant sacrifice to foreign gods. Before Moses' time, he instilled jealousy, ending in the death of individuals. During the time of Moses, the Egyptian Pharaoh's edict was to kill all Hebrew male babies. The killing of infants at the birth of Moses and the birth of Jesus attempted to stop the possibility of bringing the Messiah into this world. With these failures, Satan then turned to the destruction of the generations that God would use to fulfill the prophecy.

In our day, abortion is the tool of Satan to stop the generation that will usher in the Second Coming of our Lord. It goes even deeper than that. Please try to understand and receive the following statement: In our day, the push of those in opposition to God by encouraging abortion is satanic at its core. The reality of the death of the unborn is a demonic source of strength, for every aborted baby is a sacrifice to Satan. Their blood strengthens him. Those little ones are definitely with the Lord; I have heard them crying out to the Father, calling for justice as I engage in intercession. We know the Lord also hears their blood crying out from our ground, just as He heard Abel's blood in Genesis 4:10). May I remind you: We are in a spiritual battle for the Kingdom of God to be established on Earth as it is in Heaven.

In the introduction to this book, I shared a part of an encounter I had about God's will on earth as it is in Heaven. There is more....

After I heard the word of the Lord concerning His Book of America in Heaven, my friend who had initially asked me to pray with her on the phone screamed, "The books in Hell." With that, I looked and saw books written by Satan, containing his agenda for Earth. Again, he was copying what he knew of heaven. Satan is a counterfeiter and everything he says and does is not original. The Lord is the only one who is the true Creator. He knew that God has books in heaven written with the destiny of each individual and each nation.

My frame was not hidden from You when I was made in secret, and skillfully formed in the depths of the earth; Your eyes have seen my formless substance; and in Your book were written all the days that were ordained for me, when as yet there was not one of them.

~Psalm 139:15-16

Continuing with the vision, instantly, I saw blood pouring out of the Book of America in Heaven and knew it was the blood of the martyrs, the unborn in Heaven, and the blood of Yeshua/Jesus. As the blood fell on the books in Hell, all the words written there were washed away.

Never underestimate the power of the blood. The Blood of the Lamb is a powerful tool in our fight to overcome the enemy. The devil knows it and enlists blood for his worship also. Yet, we are not to fear. Through the blood of Yeshua/Jesus, we *are* overcomers.

And they overcame him because of the blood of the Lamb and because of the word of their testimony, and they did not love their life even when faced with death.

~ Revelation 12:11

Expressions of Replacement Theology

Once Satan came to the stark reality that the cross did not stop The Plan of God but rather upheld it, he purposed to attack the heart of God. Satan wanted to destroy His desire to bring unity and answer the prayer of Jesus in John 17: "that they may be one so the world will know You sent Me."

For those of you unfamiliar with the history of the Church from the Church fathers to the present day, you are about to see the seduction of the enemy of God on the people of God. In many cases, they genuinely loved the Lord, but through pride or offense, became captured in their understanding by the ways of Satan. It is a good lesson for us. Jesus warns us that in the end times even the elect may be deceived.

What has infected the church for nearly 1,900 years is a false doctrine that the *Church* has replaced Israel. Originally called Replacement Theology, it was introduced into the Church shortly after Gentile leadership took over from Jewish leadership. Today, we know it by other names such as Supersession or Displacement, Transfer or Fulfillment Theology.

Fulfillment Theology teaches that *Jesus Himself* fulfills all of God's promises, including His covenant with Israel; therefore, Jesus replaces Israel. Those who hold to this doctrine maintain that Israel has no theological or biblical right to exist. You see this concept in the United Nations' treatment of Israel today. It is also the basis of many denominations supporting anti-Israel practices such as the boycott of Jewish goods, the Boycott, Divestment, and Sanctions (BDS) movement.[3]

Replacement Theology, along with all its different names, except Fulfillment Theology, teaches:

1. God has rejected the Jewish people and is punishing them for rejecting Jesus as their Messiah. This teaching further states that the Jewish people are no longer God's Chosen Ones; they have lost their covenantal priority status. Jerusalem holds no place of honor or spiritual position in God. They are no different from any other people group.

Here is what God's Word has to say about that:

> *Thus says the LORD, "If My covenant for day and night stand not, and the fixed patterns of heaven and earth I have not established, then I would reject the descendants of Jacob and*

---

[3] The BDS movement is a "Hamas-inspired initiative that aims to use various forms of public protest, economic pressure, and court rulings to advance the Hamas agenda of permanently destroying Israel as a Jewish nation-state." https://www.discoverthenetworks. org/organizations/boycott-divestment-sanctions-movement-bds/

David My servant, not taking from his descendants rulers over the descendants of Abraham, Isaac and Jacob. But I will restore their fortunes and will have mercy on them."

~ Jeremiah 33:25-26

Thus says the LORD, who gives the sun for light by day and the fixed order of the moon and the stars for light by night, who stirs up the sea so that its waves roar; The LORD of hosts is His name: "If this fixed order departs from before Me," declares the LORD, "then the offspring of Israel also will cease from being a nation before Me forever."

Thus says the LORD, "If the heavens above can be measured and the foundations of the earth searched out below, then I will also cast off all the offspring of Israel for all that they have done," declares the Lord.

~ Jeremiah 31:35-37

"I say then, God has not rejected His people, has He? May it never be! For I too am an Israelite, a descendant of Abraham, of the tribe of Benjamin.

"I say then, they did not stumble so as to fall, did they? May it never be! But by their transgression salvation has come to the Gentiles, to make them jealous. Now if their transgression is riches for the world and their failure is riches for the Gentiles, how much more will their fulfillment be!"

~ Romans 11:1, 11-12

Jerusalem is the only city in the Bible that God tells us to pray for. I encourage you to do a word search on Jerusalem and see the importance of that city to the Lord.

*Pray for the peace of Jerusalem! May they prosper who love you
[the Holy City]! May peace be within your walls and prosperity
within your palaces! For my brethren and companions' sake,
I will now say, Peace be within you! For the sake of the house
of the Lord our God, I will seek, inquire for, and require your
good.*

– Psalm 122:6-9

**2. The Church is the new Israel and God is only concerned
with the Christian Church.** These maintain that Jewish people and
the land of Israel have been replaced by the Christian Church in the
purposes of God.

Sadly, they have no real understanding that the Church is more
correctly named the Ekklesia, which means a called-out assembly or
congregation. In God's relational terms, the family of God is made
up of sons and daughters through the blood of Yeshua, grafted into
the Commonwealth of Israel. How is it they keep leaving that part
out? It was stated once in Ephesians 2 and again strongly in Romans
11. As sons and daughters, we are to be the legislative body here
on Earth for our Heavenly Father to bring His Kingdom to Earth.
Throughout the Gospels, Jesus keeps saying the Kingdom is at
hand. Yes, it is, and we are God's ambassadors, fulfilling His heart's
desire and always remembering He gave us the Word of God to live
by, preserved by the Jewish people and the Jewish King Lord Jesus
to rule.

Let me repeat: God does not want everyone to be Jewish. He is
the God who created diversity. He calls for every tongue and tribe
to worship Him. He wants unity, not uniformity. Remember the
model: twelve tribes, one nation, honoring one covenant. From the
cross forward, He wants oneness.

If you learn anything from my teaching, may it be that God
gave us a model through His Word, the Jewish people, and His Son.
What is a model? It is a way to show us God's ways. Holy Spirit is

the Enabler, who helps us live out God's ways. Give room to the Holy Spirit to guide you. Stay open to His leading; He may move differently each time. The more you understand God's initial intent to receive His Word from a Hebraic perspective, you will find how often we have succumbed to replacement ideology unknowingly. The majority of denominations base their biblical understanding incorrectly which has led to a misunderstanding of Israel and God's firstborn sons and daughters. Often anti-Semitism and racism are passed down generationally through the family's iniquitous bloodline or simply through their culture.

May I encourage you to take some time with Holy Spirit and see if personal repentance is needed for yourself or stepping in the gap for your family.

> *Search me, God, and know my heart; put me to the test and know my anxious thoughts; and see if there is any hurtful way in me, and lead me in the everlasting way.*
>
> ~ Psalm 139:23-24

Taking care to intercede through repentance for yourself and your family against any roots of anti-Semitism. That intercession puts you in line for the blessing of Genesis 12.

> *"And I will bless those who bless you, and the one who curses you I will curse. And in you all the families of the earth will be blessed."*
>
> ~ Genesis 12:3

When a king sits in judgment,
he weighs all the evidence,
distinguishing the
bad from the good.

~ Proverbs 20:8, NLT

9

THE EVIDENCE

THIS CHAPTER WAS, WITHOUT a doubt, the hardest to write. Reading through the history of the evidence of Replacement Theology and the roots of anti-Semitism was very painful. Today the evidence continues in our current society globally. The opportunity to unpack the Word of God in the preceding chapters and sharing God's heart is a joy. On the contrary, the reality of man's deception and its consequences read like a horror story to me.

Living in today's world, I find the spirit of offense as the greatest tool of the enemy to bring hatred and division—in our social structures, in the workplace, and even within our families. The Bible tells us "anger gives a foothold to the devil" (Ephesians 4:27, NLT). It is offense that breeds the anger that is destroying us. Let me add that offense will negate our prayers. No matter how on target our prayers might be, God simply cannot answer them if we are holding some offense in our hearts. Our adversary, the devil, the accuser of the brethren, will be quick to point out that sin to the Father and remind Him that He cannot respond to our prayers.

Sadly, nothing has changed since the beginning of time as we know it. We discussed earlier in this book how in Ephesians 2 that offense became a dividing wall that Yeshua/Jesus had to bring down between the Jewish people and the Gentiles.

Offense—either causing it or receiving it from someone else—is a strategy of the enemy we can all fall prey to. God is clear that we are not to judge one another, but to walk in love one to another. Certainly, believers are not to compromise truth; we need to have a voice in these critical times. However, we must speak truth with God's purpose, not to argue a point. It is a fine line, indeed, to be led of the Spirit, and a great deal of intercession is needed. *Our* words, as well as our intercession, must come from the throne of God—generated by *His* Word, clothed in humility, and empowered with the anointing. All this must be founded on the love of God shed abroad in our hearts by the Holy Spirit (Romans 5:5b, KJV).

Martin Luther's Changing View
of the Jewish People

Before we study a timeline of the historic evidence of anti-Semitism and Replacement Theology allow me to point out one of the most powerful examples of carrying an offense that is recorded in our Church history.

Martin Luther was used mightily by God to bring reformation to the Church, and yet he became one of the most influential anti-Semites of all time. How is it possible for a lover of Christ to turn on the people God loves and the natural bloodline from which God's Son comes?

This is a serious warning to the Church because we can trace Luther's influence through the Holocaust.

Martin Luther began his adult life pursuing a law degree to please his father. In 1505, he was caught in a terrible storm and cried out to the patron saint of miners, St. Anne, to save him. His prayer was sealed with a commitment that if she answered, he would become a monk. Historians believe this was something he had been thinking about and this event sealed the deal. It is said Luther was driven by fear of hell and God's wrath—a telling statement. The motivation of fear cannot produce the intimate relationship with our God that sent His Son to die for us. If we are in relationship with God, waiting for Him to drop the other shoe, where is the place for His transforming love in our life?

As a monk, Luther was given an opportunity to be a delegate to a conference by the Catholic Church in Rome. He came back, discouraged by the actions of the priests concerning morality and the great corruption in the Church.

Our current headlines show us much of what Luther encountered still has a foothold in the hierarchy of the Catholic Church. A great many Catholics today have a true passion for the Lord and His ways. In many communities across the USA, they are leading the charge *against* abortion and *for* the preservation of the family. However, when anything contrary to God's principles is kept in the dark, it cannot be reformed. Light is the only thing that can dispel the darkness in a community or an individual.

Luther's disappointment with what he encountered motivated him to change direction and attend the University of Wittenberg, where he received a doctorate as a professor of theology. Around 1515, through his studies, he realized the key to salvation was not fear but faith, and through that revelation, the Reformation began.

As I continued to research Luther's story, I came to believe his understanding of faith did not hold the depth of God's love needed to heal his brokenness. Read on and consider how important it is not only to hear the truth of God's love but also to let that truth become the foundation of your walk with Him.

Early in his career, Luther had a love for the Jewish people. In 1523, he wrote an essay, "That Jesus Christ Was Born a Jew." In this piece, he stated: "If I had been a Jew and had seen such dolts and blockheads govern and teach Christian Faith, I would sooner have become a hog than a Christian. They have dealt with the Jews as if they were dogs rather than human beings; they have done little else than deride them and seize their property.... If the apostles, who were Jews, had dealt with us Gentiles as we Gentiles deal with the Jews, there would never have been a Christian among the Gentiles.... When we are inclined to boast of our position as Christians, we should remember that we are but Gentiles, while the Jews are of the lineage of Christ."[1]

However, in 1543, when Luther was unsuccessful in bringing the Jews to their Messiah, he denounced them and called for harsh persecution of followers of Judaism. In an essay entitled "On the Jews and Their Lies,"[2] he wrote: "What shall we Christians do with this rejected and condemned people the Jews?"

The derogatory things he said directly about them are crass, and I choose not to repeat them. However, you can easily find them on the internet in the writings I have cited. The following are only a few suggestions Luther made to the Christians to harass the Jews:

- Set fires to their synagogues and schools in the honor of our Lord.

- Raze and destroy their houses.

- Take away their prayer books and Talmudic writings which are lies, cursing, and blasphemy.

---

[1] Martin Luther, "That Jesus Christ was Born a Jew," Trans. Walter I Brandt, in Luther's Works (Philadelphia: Fortress Press, 1962), 200-201, 229.

[2] Martin Luther, "On the Jews and Their Lies," https://ml33.ams3.digitaloceanspaces.com/home/admin/web/martyleeds33.com/public_html/2021/01/Martin-Luther-on-the-Jew-and-their-Lies.pdf

- Forbid their rabbis to teach or they shall have loss of life and limb.[3]

So, what happened? A spirit of offense rose up in Luther because he could not convert the Jewish people. His love of God was eventually drowned out by pride and ambition. Could it have been that his understanding was merely intellectual, based on reading the Word of God rather than truly heartfelt, enabling him to see with God's perspective?

In 1522, history records that after he was excommunicated by the Catholic Church, he began Lutheranism in Germany, found favor with the German prince, and gained many followers. In 1524, however, the peasants revolted, and he denounced them. While thousands were killed in that revolt, Luther grew his church. And therein lies the problem, for the work of the Kingdom is not ours but God's, and growing a church or a ministry should be the work of the Holy Spirit, not an instrument to destroy lives.

For all Luther's contributions to the Protestant Reformation, he did not finish well.

Gentile Church Fathers

Paul's warnings to the Church to stay true to the plan of God concerning the Jewish people are clear. (We covered those warnings in Chapter 7: "Level Playing Field," citing Romans 9-11, which according to my research, was written in A.D. 58. It seems that trouble was already brewing against the plan of God, and Paul took the time to set the record straight.

From Church history, let us track the positions of Gentile theologians considered to be respected Church fathers. I present

[3] Robert Michael, Holy Hatred: Christianity, Antisemitism, and the Holocaust (New York: Palgrave McMillan, 2006).

Justin Martyr in greater detail than the other theologians since I feel he laid the groundwork for the others.

Justin Martyr—By A.D. 150, Justin Martyr, a Samaritan believer, became the first to lay the foundation of Replacement Theology in his paper, "Dialogue with Trypho."[4]

He has two works still considered genuine: "Apologies"[5] and "Dialogue with Trypho"

Trypho was a learned Jew and this document was intended by Martyr to defend Christianity to him. Before I share the basis of his theses, let me tell you about Justin's background and theology. Justin was raised as a pagan in a Jewish environment. He studied many pagan philosophies before he became a Christian around 132. By 135 he began traveling to share his newfound faith in hopes of converting educated pagans. Eventually, he was considered a revolutionary by a Roman prefect and condemned to death.

In the first part of "First Apology," Justin defends his fellow Christian against atheism and hostility to Rome. He clarifies his Christian philosophy by stating that both Christianity and Platonic philosophy are in agreement of an unchangeable God. And that intellectual articulation of the Christian faith would demonstrate its harmony with reason. Stating that such convergence is rooted in the relationship between human reason and the divine mind. Thus, he makes the argument that intellect will enable man to understand basic truths about the world, time, creation, freedom, and the human soul's relationship with a divine spirit and be able to recognize good and evil.

He goes on to say that Jesus Christ is the incarnation of the divine intellect and, where only traces of this belief were found in pagan philosophy, Justin taught that the purpose of Christ coming

---

[4]Justin Martyr, https://earlychurch.org.uk/pdf/e-books/williams_a-lukyn/dialogue-with-trypho_williams.pdf.

[5]Justin Martyr, http://media.bloomsbury.com/rep/files/primary-source-31-justin-martyr.pdf.

into the world was to teach men the truth and to save them from the power of demons.

Really? I thought His coming was to pay the price for our sin and to deliver us unto eternal life. It was to give us a revelation of the Father and His great love for us. Yeshua/Jesus came to redeem man's fall through Adam and make a way to restore the fellowship in the Garden that God intended us to have eternally.

Do you see it? Here is the basis of Greek thinking creeping into the foundation of the Church as opposed to the Hebraic mindset, which is based on relationship thinking. Through His Word, God continually reveals who He is; intellect alone cannot define Him.

> *"For My thoughts are not your thoughts, nor are your ways My ways," says the Lord. "For as the heavens are higher than the earth, so are My ways higher than your ways, and My thoughts than your thoughts."*
>
> ~ Isaiah 55:8-9

Can you wrap your intellect around Noah and the ark, the virgin birth, or the miracles of Yeshua/Jesus or those in the Old Testament? I can't. It is only faith that gives credibility, so you know that you know the truth about the Father and His Son.

Am I saying that God did not give us the intelligence to understand science and the natural world around us? No, I am saying our salvation is based on a relationship with the God of the universe and we cannot understand Him without His Spirit leading us into all truth.

Here is what God tells us about the intellect of man:

> *For the story and message of the cross is sheer absurdity and folly to those who are perishing and on their way to perdition, but to us who are being saved it is the [manifestation of] the power of God. For it is written, I will baffle and render useless and*

destroy the learning of the learned and the philosophy of the philosophers and the cleverness of the clever and the discernment of the discerning; I will frustrate and nullify [them] and bring [them] to nothing. Where is the wise man (the philosopher)? Where is the scribe (the scholar)? Where is the investigator (the logician, the debater) of this present time and age? Has not God shown up the nonsense and the folly of this world's wisdom? For when the world with all its earthly wisdom failed to perceive and recognize and know God by means of its own philosophy, God in His wisdom was pleased through the foolishness of preaching [salvation, procured by Christ and to be had through Him], to save those who believed (who clung to and trusted in and relied on Him). For while Jews [demandingly] ask for signs and miracles and Greeks pursue philosophy and wisdom, we preach Christ (the Messiah) crucified, [preaching which] to the Jews is a scandal and an offensive stumbling block [that springs a snare or trap], and to the Gentiles it is absurd and utterly unphilosophical nonsense. But to those who are called, whether Jew or Greek (Gentile), Christ [is] the Power of God and the Wisdom of God. [This is] because the foolish thing [that has its source in] God is wiser than men, and the weak thing [that springs] from God is stronger than men.

~ 1 Corinthians 1:18-25, AMP

I have a confession to make. I did not receive Yeshua/Jesus into my life because of the knowledge that He died for me. Hear me: I am not saying the Word of God is not powerful. But without the anointing on it, it is just words. Mere words alone did not capture my heart; it was the presence of the Lord through His Spirit that drew me to Him. Yeshua/Jesus clearly said several times only by the Spirit can we know him.

He said to them, "But who do you say that I am?" Simon Peter answered and said, "You are the Christ, the Son of the living God." Jesus answered and said to him, "Blessed are you, Simon

Bar-Jonah, for flesh and blood has not revealed this to you, but My Father who is in heaven.

~ Matthew 16:15-17

"God is Spirit, and those who worship Him must worship in spirit and truth."

~ John 4:24

In fact, all the truth in the Bible did not make an impact on me until after I was saved. So why do I love Him? I do, I just do. It is a Spirit-to-spirit thing that I can barely explain. Now that I know the Lord, the Word is exciting and my times with Him are rich and full.

Now, as I study the history of the Church, it seems that many of those who are coming to faith through intellect only are being used by Satan to bring division and pain to the Body of Christ and the apple of His eye, the Jewish people. The Greek mindset has permeated the doctrine of the Church throughout history and remains in some ways subtle and, in other ways, overt in overriding the true heart of God.

In his book, *The Messianic Church Arising*, Robert Heidler addresses the issue of what happened when the early Church fathers incorporated pagan thinking, or Greek mindset, with the Word of God: "According to the Bible, salvation comes by 'believing in' Jesus. When this was reinterpreted through the intellectual Greek mindset, the wording changed from 'believing in' to 'believing that' certain doctrines are true. This small change in wording had enormous implications. Salvation was redefined as an intellectual agreement with a set of doctrines."[6]

As you study the thought patterns of many Gentile Church fathers after the apostles, you see just how dangerous that "small change" was.

[6] Heidler, The Messianic Church Arising.

So, in the "Dialogue with Trypho," Justin tries to prove the truth to this learned Jew that a new covenant has superseded the old covenant of God with the Jewish people. That Yeshua/Jesus is both the Messiah announced in the Old Testament and God revealed Himself in the Scriptures. He goes on to state that Gentiles have been chosen to replace Israel as God's chosen people. His concept is of a divine plan as a process of salvation integrated into history as a unity directed supernaturally with an end to bring the Old Testament and Greek philosophy into a meeting to form a single stream of Christianity. Within the writings of this work, he makes it clear that he feels the Jews have lost the title Israel; true Israel are the Gentile Christians. He even states that Jewish physical circumcision is a sign of God's judgment.

To understand how Justin twisted the Word of God to defend his thoughts, here is a direct quote about circumcision found in Chapter 16 of a book titled *The Ante-Nicene Fathers.*[7]

"For the circumcision according to the flesh, which is from Abraham, was given for a sign that you may be separated from other nations, and from us; and that you might suffer that which you now justly suffer; and that your land may be desolate, and your cities burned with fire; and that strangers may eat your fruit in your presence, and not one of you may go up to Jerusalem."

It has been said the word taken out of context can be used to defend whatever you want it to. The above is a perfect example.

His statement on the New Covenant has been used widely to misrepresent the Lord. Here in the book of Jeremiah we see that the New Covenant was given specifically to the Jewish people. The words New Covenant first appears in the Word in this Scripture:

Behold, the days are coming, says the LORD, when I will make
a new covenant with the house of Israel and with the house

---

[7] William B. Eerdmans, The Ante-Nicene Fathers, (Grand Rapids: Wm. B. Edermans Publishing Company, 1975), 73.

of Judah, Not according to the covenant which I made with their fathers in the day when I took them by the hand to bring them out of the land of Egypt, My covenant which they broke, although I was their Husband, says the LORD. But this is the covenant which I will make with the house of Israel: After those days, says the LORD, I will put My law within them, and on their hearts will I write it; and I will be their God, and they will be My people.

~ Jeremiah 31:31-33

In Luke 22:20, at the Passover, Yeshua/Jesus is talking with His twelve Jewish apostles who would remember that the words new covenant first appeared in Jeremiah and were spoken to Israel and the Jewish people by the Lord. As grafted in believers, this covenant applies to you.

At that Passover, when Yeshua/Jesus says, this is "My blood shed for you," He is making clear that the act of shedding His blood will be the fulfillment of the New Covenant in Jeremiah 31.

Now later in Jeremiah, the Lord states:

Thus says the LORD: If the heavens above can be measured and the foundations of the earth searched out beneath, then I will cast off all the offspring of Israel for all that they have done, says the LORD.

~ Jeremiah 31:37

This Scripture affirms that nothing this people can do can remove this covenant. That kind of seals the deal and blows holes in Justin's argument.

If you have come this far in reading this book, you will see how the chapter entitled "Great Deception" (Chapter 8) had its foundation. Modern Replacement Theology uses Justin Martyr's thesis for their biblical stand, which is not at all biblical. Sadly, many denominational churches hold fast to this wrong thinking.

To add insult to injury, within a few years, A.D. 175, Pope Victor of Rome became famous as the priest who condemned the use of biblical feasts on the Jewish calendar. This is no small thing as the Bible tells us in Daniel 7:25:

> *And he shall speak words against the Most High [God] and shall wear out the saints of the Most High and think to change the time [of sacred feasts and holy days] and the law; and the saints shall be given into his hand for a time, two times, and half a time [three and one-half years].*
>
> ~ Daniel 7:25, AMPC

The appointed times of the Lord have great value. God made it very clear that even after King Jesus has taken His seat in Jerusalem, the earth will continue to celebrate them.

Origen (A.D. 185-254)—Considered an important influencer of the Christian Church. It is said of him that he tried to pull together Neoplatonism and Stoicism with Christianity. To do so, he spiritualized the Word of God, using ideology contrary to the Word, and continued as Justin Martyr to promote the idea that the Church replaced Israel. In his work against Celsus, he made his case against the Jews with such statements as "the Jews, killers of God." A term I (Joanie) grew up with was "Christ-killers." He stated God would punish them forever.

By A.D. 306, nineteen bishops and twenty-six presbyters gathered in Elvia, a province of Rome, now southern Spain. This synod forbade Christians to marry Jews, to receive prayers from them, or even to eat with them. This root of anti-Semitism is probably why Jews were expelled from Spain later in history.

Constantine (A.D. 272-337)—We first hear of the Emperor Constantine, who convened the Council of Nicea in A.D. 325. He is described as an unbaptized catechumen—one who is trained in the Christian faith for the purpose of baptism. Interestingly he was not baptized.

This First Council of Nicaea called by Constantine was to solve the problem created by Arius of Alexandria that affirmed that Christ was not divine but a created being. The council condemned Arius and signified the absolute equality of the Son with the Father. They tried to establish a uniform date for Easter but failed. It is significant to point out that Easter is not biblical. They also tried to put in many laws of how to operate in the Christian church including making a canon to enforce celibacy but failed. Here it is clear how the doctrines of men are counter to the Word of God. Man's doctrine is not only found among Christian writings. Rabbi scholars have also imposed man-made doctrines in the writings of the Talmud, which are commentaries on the Torah that hold great weight in the Jewish community.

Easter is an exceptionally good example of how the mixture of pagan beliefs infiltrated God's original purposes. The early Church kept Passover with an understanding that Yeshua/Jesus was, in fact, the Passover Lamb and that God instituted that feast to not only remember the great deliverance He brought the Israelites through but to point to the ultimate deliverance Yeshua/Jesus would provide through His death and resurrection for all mankind. He rose on the Feast of First Fruits, three days after the Passover, becoming the first fruits of those raised from the dead to eternal life.

Constantine changed the celebrations of Passover to a celebration of new life, which aligned with the first full moon following the spring equinox. The name Easter comes from a goddess called *Eostre*, known as a fertility goddess and celebrated at the beginning of spring. Since Exodus 12 gives us the date and *precise* instructions from God to celebrate Passover, this is a clear picture of the evil intent of Satan to pervert the ways of the Lord.

With additional church councils through the years, Constantine made many hurtful changes to the Church. He removed all Hebraic teachings by forbidding the celebration of all feasts, including Sabbath. He mingled worship and teaching with paganism. Combining what God gave as His model to the early Church with pagan ways broke down the foundation of the Church. Much has been written about Constantine. (For further information, see Suggested Readings in this book.)

Saint John Chrysostom (A.D. 344-407)—In his eight "Homilies Against the Jews,"[8] he tried to create fear and disgust toward the Jewish people to keep his parishioners away from the Jewish people, fearing they would leave Christianity. After Augustine, he was the most popular with the Reformers. Sadly, today he is still regarded with honor, and in some denominations, much of Replacement Theology finds its substance in his writings.

Augustine of Hippo (A.D. 354-430)—Considered one of the most important developers in Western Christianity, Augustine is credited as the founder of theology by both Roman Catholic and Protestant theologians. It is stated of him he joined Neoplatonism and Plato's doctrines with Christianity.

Augustine believed that the contemporary Byzantine Church was allegorically speaking of the millennial reign of Christ on Earth. He saw the Jewish people and their sufferings as God-ordained and a witness that Israel exists to testify to its own wickedness. He saw their irrevocable calling as punishment, not preeminence. Therefore, his teaching led many to believe that they should cooperate with God to bring miseries upon the Jewish people. It is stated that he did have other literature calling on Gentile Christians to preach to

---

8 John Chrysostom, Homilies Against the Jews, https://www.colchestercollection.com/titles/pdf/E/eight-homilies.pdf.

the Jews in the spirit of love, but those writings did not get the same representation to the people as the hatred literature.

Moving Forward

I have given you an overview of the foundational principles used to discredit God's heart and ways as revealed in His Word. Those faulty foundations have been built upon through the ages in the Church. It's a wonder we ever had the opportunity to know the whole truth! Yet, in God's mercy, many are coming to understand and rediscover their intended inheritance through the Hebraic mindset. Biblical Hebrew study opens up a depth of understanding of the majesty and deep treasures of love and wisdom of our God. Viewing life through a Hebraic mindset brings us a richness in relationship with each other and our God as we begin to grasp the mysteries of His Word.

I often hear from those who have joined the journey of discovery that the big picture has finally taken on substance. They say individual pieces of truth come together through their new lens of study.

Today, outside the Church structure, anti-Semitism finds its demonstration in several ways. You find it in Communism, globalism, Islam, and the ever-rising socialism movement attempting to invade America. We see the anti-Israel sentiment throughout all the political structures here in the USA and other nations growing at an alarming rate. Sadly, those same anti-Israel sentiments are deeply entrenched within the Church structure as well. We see that evidence as denominations withdraw their support for Israel financially.

The political and religious spirits have joined hands to bring destruction to Israel and the world as we know it. Yet that is nothing new. They were working in Yeshua's/Jesus' time as well to destroy the work of the cross and Kingdom-building.

Have you ever wondered why most Jewish people feel that believing in Yeshua/Jesus is a betrayal to their Judaism? Especially since Yeshua/Jesus is Jewish and followed the Jewish way of life.

Satan has used the Church throughout history to destroy the Jews. We are most familiar with the Crusades and in our generation the Holocaust, which was presented to the Jewish as an act of obedience to Christ. However, if you want a detailed story of all the ways the Jewish people have been scared, I recommend Dr. Howard Morgan's book *So Deeply Scared.*[9]

Let me take you a step further back and show you how I believe the political and religious spirit put a curse on my people.

We have read how the Church has removed the Hebraic root of God's intent. Let me show you how the rabbinic community wanted to separate the Jewish believers from their heritage. The following is what I believe might have been an underlying reason. A thought process infused in the leadership by religious and political spirits. The Jews were accepted by the governmental structure of their time and given special dispensation to not have to worship the other gods of the general public. There was a great concern among the leaders that this new sect of Judaism, the Messianic believers, would jeopardize the political status of the established Jews. In an attempt to separate believers and non-believers who were both worshiping in the temple together, there was a prayer introduced into the liturgy called the Amidah still part of the service today. The prayer (Birkat HaMinim,[10] benediction of the apostates) calls for the destruction of apostates which are considered the Jewish followers of Yeshua/Jesus. The prayer contained a curse that the Jewish followers of Yeshua/Jesus would perish and be blotted from the book of the living. Knowing what we know in the power of words, I have to think that

[9] See Suggested Readings

[10] Birkat HaMinim, the benediction of the apostates. https://jewsforjesus.org/jewish-resources/messianic-jews-a-brief-history/.

in part this is responsible for the Jewish people having such a strong aversion to accepting their Messiah.

Not sharing Yeshua/Jesus with my people to me is the greatest form of anti-Semitism that the devil has produced. To be clear, Yeshua/Jesus is the only way to the Father. To not share that truth is Satan's cruel tool to separate the Jewish people from God for eternity. It takes wisdom to present the Gospel to them because of their history of persecution. Unfortunately, many words trigger a negative response in their emotions. The name Yeshua/Jesus is a curse to them. Holocaust survivors recount they were told that it was in the name of Yeshua/Jesus that the Germans were instructed to persecute them. In Spain's history, the Jewish people were told if they didn't convert to Christianity, they would lose their lives. So, when presenting biblical truths to my people, a sensitive vocabulary is important. Written by Sid Roth with other leaders, the book *Time Is Running Short* is a helpful guide. This book, along with others, is found in Suggested Readings.

My hope is that as I have shared what I have learned over the last 20 years, it will inspire you to take your own journey of discovery. If I have touched on places that have caused you to want to know more, then this book has accomplished its purpose. Understanding your Hebraic foundation is a lifelong journey, but trust me—it is worth the effort.

There is so much more I long to share with you. At the end of this book, there are listed some excellent resources from other authors that express my heart. Their books will not only inform you about the history of the Jewish people but current events too. Many of the authors I am honored to call friends. I encourage you to take advantage of their scholarship.

Enjoy the journey!

Love,

Joanie

SUGGESTED READING

These books can be ordered through most online retailers or directly from the authors' websites.

Apostolic Church Arising by Chuck Pierce and Robert Heidler

The Messianic Church Arising: Restoring the Church to Our Covenant Roots! by Robert Heidler

Possessing Your Inheritance: Moving Forward in God's Covenant Plan for Your Life
by Chuck Pierce and Rebecca Wagner Systema
(Also available at www.store.gloryofzion.org/collections/books)

Activating the Prophetic by Clay Nash

Relational Authority; Authentic Leadership by Clay Nash
(Also available at www.claynash.org.)

Israel: The Key to World Revival by Avner Boskey
(Also available on the author's website: www.davidstent.org/books)

Why Care About Israel? by Sandra Teplinsky

Why Still Care About Israel? by Sandra Teplinsky

Israel's Anointing: Your Inheritance and End-Time Destiny through Israel by Sandra Teplinsky
(Also available at www.lightofzion.org/books-2/)

Your People Shall Be My People: How Israel, the Jews and the Christian Church Will Come Together in the Last Days (updated and expanded edition) by Don Finto

(Also available at www.donfinto.org)

The Coming Israel Awakening: Gazing into the Future of the Jewish People and the Church by James Goll

Praying for Israel's Destiny by James Goll

(Also available at www.godencounters.com)

The Incomplete Church by Sid Roth

They Thought for Themselves by Sid Roth

(Also available at www.sidroth.org)

So Deeply Scared by Dr. Howard Morgan

(Only available at www.kingmin.org)

The Hiding Place by Corrie Ten Boom

Tramp for the Lord by Corrie Ten Boom

New Era Glory: Stepping into God's Accelerated Season of Outpouring and Breakthrough by Tim Sheets

(Also available at www.tim-sheets-ministries.myshopify.com)

His Appointed Times: Hebrew/Gregorian Calendar by Christine Vales

(Also available at www.christinevales.com)

BOOKS ON REACHING THE JEWISH PEOPLE

For the Sake of the Fathers: A New Testament View of God's Love for the Jewish People by David Harwood

Christianity Is Jewish by Edith Schaeffer

Time is Running Short by Sid Roth
(Also available at www.sidroth.org)

BOOKS ON PRAYER

Intercessory Prayer: How God Can Use Your Prayers to Move Heaven and Earth by Dutch Sheets

Watchman Prayer by Dutch Sheets
(Also available at www.dutchsheets.org)

Praying for Israel's Destiny by James Goll

A more detailed book reading list and articles by the
author (under the name Hadasah) are available on the
One in Messiah Ministries' website:
WWW.OIMM.ORG

About The Author

Joan Masterson is an author and teacher, revealing the prophetic significance of the Hebrew foundations of our faith and the plan closest to God's heart - the One New Man. She is the author, most recently, of Dwelling Place. Under the pen name of Melody Hope, she has authored a series of children's books, "The Jeremy Series", inspiring character, creativity, and confidence.

As the founder of One in Messiah Ministries, she regularly writes for the OIMM website (www.oimm.org), nationally facilitates home Shabbat and Rosh Chodesh fellowships, as well as regional gatherings to celebrate the Feasts of the Lord. As a teacher, she has been on many public platforms and taught for five years at Caleb Global. One of her greatest joys as a teacher is her interactive national call-in class operating now for over 25 years on Biblical Hebraic topics.

Joan is ordained by Dr. Howard Morgan - Kingdom Ministries Interational. One in Messiah Ministries is commissioned by Chuck Pierce and Glory of Zion International.

Also Available

The Jeremy Series....

Jeremy's birthday has arrived and this birthday is special because he's moving from his crib to his first big-boy bed. *The Birthday Quilt* is a heartwarming story filled with the sounds of life, the excitement of transition and a special mystery. Extra bonus family fun guide accompanies this book with projects the whole family can enjoy.

The Birthday Quilt

Available at
Amazon.com | Barnes & Noble.com | Walmart.com | Target.com

What are you thankful for? How do you bless others? Join Jeremy's family as they put principle into practice and open their home to a family in need. Faith meets works, creating hope in *Thank You Saturday*. Family fun guide included.

Thank You Saturday

Available at
Amazon.com | Barnes & Noble.com | Walmart.com | Target.com

Jeremy's Scarecrow
A Tikvah Storybook

Story by
Melody Hope

Illustrations by
Laurie Wong

Jeremy's Scarecrow is a story written for you and your child to explore the importance and rewards of friendship and the need for patience while learning to wait. This book also contains a family fun guide with a project the whole family will enjoy.

Jeremy's Scarecrow

Available at
Amazon.com I Barnes & Noble.com I Walmart.com I Target.com

LEAVE A REVIEW

If you enjoyed this book, will you please consider writing a review on Amazon and Goodreads. Reviews help authors make their books more visible to new readers.

CONNECT WITH THE AUTHOR

Facebook:
Facebook.com/joanmastersonauthor

Instagram:
Instagram.com/joaniemasterson

Goodreads:
Goodreads.com/joanmasterson

XAPit:
Xapit.com/page/joan-masterson

Email:
joanie@joanmasterson.com

Join the conversation on social media
by using the hashtag:
#onenewman or #dwellingplace

Would you like Joan to speak
at your church or event?

Contact:
Joanie@JoanMasterson.com

www.JoanMasterson.com

CPSIA information can be obtained
at www.ICGtesting.com
Printed in the USA
JSHW012005180123
36467JS00001B/52